In Plain Sight

In Plain Sight

Simple, Difficult Lessons from New Jersey's Expensive Effort to Close the Achievement Gap

Gordon MacInnes

A Century Foundation Book

2009 • The Century Foundation Press • New York

LIBRARY OF CONGRESS CATALOGING-IN-PUBLICATION DATA

MacInnes, Gordon, 1941-
  In plain sight : simple, difficult lessons from New Jersey's expensive effort to close the achievement gap / Gordon MacInnes.
    p. cm.
  Includes bibliographical references.
  ISBN 978-0-87078-513-9
  1. Educational equalization–New Jersey. 2. Education and state–New Jersey. 3. School improvement programs–New Jersey. 4. Academic achievement–New Jersey. I. Title.

LC213.22.N5M33 2008
379.2'6–dc22

2008048746

Manufactured in the United States of America.
Cover design: Claude Goodwin
Cover photo: Randall Hagadorn, by permission of the Educational Testing Service.

FOREWORD

Most Americans share the conviction that a significant portion of the success of individuals will vary according to the quality and quantity of their educational attainment. Lifetime income is, in fact, closely correlated with educational achievement. Business has institutionalized this relationship by making education the touchstone of hiring, promotion, and even plant location policies. Education, not surprisingly, is one of the few domestic governmental activities endorsed by virtually all elements in the political spectrum. Even taxes, the bane of every officeholder's existence, sometimes can be justified if tied to the needs of education.

By the time they reach secondary school, over 90 percent of American students are in public schools, managed by 14,561 different school districts. Public education, however, is not without its critics—a chorus that has been growing larger and more insistent over the past few decades. While it is true that most public school parents are satisfied with the education their children receive, it is simultaneously the case that challenges to the public school system are under way in every state, and that claims that the public schools are failing broadly are commonplace. The well-off vote with their feet, by competing fiercely for places in highly priced and highly prized private schools, or moving to affluent, homogenous suburbs. Others, adhering to religious or personal beliefs, insist that alternate schools—at home or in non-secular institutions—are better for their offspring. And, a movement encompassing charter schools and vouchers is based on the notion that existing public school establishments will not and perhaps cannot change enough to meet the needs of many children.

Still, despite a growing interest in an enlarged federal role in elementary and secondary education, the system remains overwhelmingly in the hands of state and local governments and school districts. In national political and education circles, of course, a lively and intense debate swirls about the impact of the federal law popularly know as No Child Left Behind (NCLB). In brief, the goal of this law is to improve the education of large numbers of children by increasing the accountability of their teachers and school administrators. Although federal education spending covers less than one-tenth of the total cost of public elementary and secondary education in the United States, it is believed that this money, on a margin, can shape the behavior and effect the enhancement of educational professionals, particularly those who actually manage education at the state and local level. But while NCLB has received enormous attention, it is clear that the main decisions about education have taken place with state and local governments.

The primacy of state government responsibility for education is written into many state constitutions. In New Jersey, the state is required to provide "for the maintenance and support of a thorough and efficient system of free public schools." This clause and others like it in other states have led to a series of landmark legal cases across the country, redefining the role that states—already dominant in school policy—must play in ensuring school quality.

In New Jersey, these cases have driven the debate and policies about education for more than forty years. New Jersey State Supreme Court decisions (*Robinson* v. *Cahill* and the numerous iterations of *Abbott* v. *Burke*) have required the state to finance a greater share of the cost of K–12 education in districts that have significant numbers of students from low-income families. One effect of this trend is that an ever-growing share of state aid has gone to the so-called Abbott districts. The implications of these financial and educational policies have been so significant that public education controversies have been the major force shaping overall politics for a generation. The court, for example, has prodded the state to increase tax revenues, even closing the public schools briefly in 1976 when the state failed to enact new taxes required to fund a new school aid formula.

Indeed, New Jersey political actors have come to accept as normal these frequent and complex court mandates in the area of education—mandates that, in effect, set the agenda for the state legislature and the governor. Over the same period, on several occasions, the state has stepped in and taken over the direct management of certain urban school districts, a process that continues to this day.

There is a great deal to learn, both good and bad, from the New Jersey experience and there is no one better to tell that story than Gordon MacInnes. It is no exaggeration to say that he knows the issues, the facts, and the implications of the struggle to close the achievement gap in New Jersey's public schools better than anyone else. He served as a staff member responsible for education, among other things, for Governor Richard J. Hughes; worked closely with several state education commissioners; served in the New Jersey Assembly and Senate; and spent five years as New Jersey's assistant commissioner for education, responsible for the Division of Abbott Implementation.

As MacInnes's work makes clear, the lessons derived from four decades of "school reform" in New Jersey have meaningful implications for these issues elsewhere. Wherever there are vexing and persistent gaps between the performances of poor children and those from well-off families—and these gaps exist across the nation—then the New Jersey experience is relevant.

In Plain Sight: Simple Difficult Lessons from New Jersey's Expensive Effort to Close the Achievement Gap serves as a nice complement to The Century Foundation's major focus on the area of K–12 education over the past decade: reducing concentrations of school poverty. Several of our publications, including senior fellow Richard D. Kahlenberg's *All Together Now: Creating Middle-Class Schools through Public School Choice* (2001); and the report of The Century Foundation's education task force, *Divided We Fail: Coming Together through Public School Choice* (2002), make a strong case that the single best action that can be taken to improve the lot of low-income students is to provide them with good middle-class schools—where teachers are highly qualified and have high expectations, parents actively volunteer in the school and hold officials accountable, and peers provide an environment that is supportive of educational achievement. But it is not always politically or logistically possible to create socioeconomically integrated schools, and MacInnes's book provides hope about what can be accomplished, even in schools with very high concentrations of poverty.

In Plain Sight is remarkably frank and comprehensive in its assessment of what has worked and what has not. It provides specific answers to the question of why some districts have been more successful than others in closing the achievement gap. While rigorous in his use of facts, MacInnes is obviously no Ivory Tower observer—he provides an on-the-ground assessment that is invaluable. On behalf of the Trustees of The Century Foundation, I thank Gordon MacInnes for his efforts.

RICHARD C. LEONE, PRESIDENT
THE CENTURY FOUNDATION
December 2008

CONTENTS

1

INTRODUCTION

This is a story about what happens when a state education department partners with city school districts in an attempt to close the achievement gap between poor, minority city students and their counterparts in the predominantly white and more affluent suburban districts. It is a story set in New Jersey, but the lessons apply in any American city that has concentrations of poor children in failing school districts. The pedagogical puzzles that must be solved in Gary or El Paso vary not at all from those in Camden or Elizabeth. What sets New Jersey apart is the generous level of court-mandated funding available, and the fact that preschool in the state begins at age three.

New Jersey's experience presents a test to determine if more money produces better results. A preliminary look at the results of the state's efforts suggests an unsurprising conclusion: when additional funds are concentrated on supporting and enhancing teachers' efforts to assess the needs of their students and tailor their instruction to those needs, dramatically better results are possible. If no coherent plan for improved classroom instruction is implemented, more money makes no difference, and can, instead, produce confusion and declining performance.

New Jersey has demonstrated remarkable success in improving children's educational attainment. For example, only in Massachusetts did fourth graders score higher than those in New Jersey, a much more diverse state, on the 2007 National Assessment of Educational Progress

(NAEP) reading test.[1] Between the 2005 and 2007 tests, New Jersey fourth grade scores improved by eight scale points overall, and those of African Americans went up by twelve and those of Latinos increased by eight. New Jersey was the only state in which scores in all ethnic categories improved over 2005.[2] It is the contention of this book that New Jersey's fairly dramatic improvement is a product of a focused effort by many of New Jersey's poorest school districts to introduce effective early literacy practices.[3]

Politicians, scholars, business leaders, educators, and advocates for one point of view or another have conducted a largely fruitless debate for four decades about the achievement gap. Mostly, it has been a discussion among people who have very little appreciation for what it means to face a class of twenty-five eight-year-olds six hours a day for 180 days a year. The policy debates produce a seemingly endless list of proposed solutions that are irrelevant to the conditions and opportunities in that second grade classroom.

The obvious truth is that the transactions between millions of poor minority children and thousands of teachers are not working. In 2007, 54 percent of black and 51 percent of Latino students nationally scored below "basic" on the NAEP fourth grade reading test, while only 14 percent of black students and 17 percent of Latinos were "proficient" or "advanced proficient" (compared to 42 percent for white students).[4] We must focus on how to change what takes place in the classrooms of these students. This is not an issue that can be solved simply by new policy—the assumption all along has been that schools must teach children how to read—it is an issue of will and practice.

The story in New Jersey assumes that most agree on the initial causes of the achievement gap—social class and early-life language acquisition. A five-year-old from a lower-class family starts kindergarten without enough vocabulary and general knowledge to be ready to begin reading and writing in first grade. Most schools do not know how to close this kindergarten gap and, if they do not, most of their kindergarten "graduates" will never be strong readers. At least that is the record of the last forty years or so.

A second assumption is that the students who are not confident readers by the end of third grade—certainly by fourth grade—are pretty much doomed. When schools relied on dumbed-down textbooks, poor minority students struggled; but the introduction of new, tougher academic standards only exacerbates an already discouraging achievement gap. The 2007 NAEP eighth grade reading test showed that nationwide, while 38 percent of white students were proficient or advanced proficient, only 12 percent of black and 14 percent of Latinos were.[5]

So this is a story that concentrates on children from age three through third grade. For poor minority children who go to school with other poor minority children (and most do), their best opportunity to use education to move into the middle class pretty much ends at age nine. As troubling as that may seem, educators know how to do the work to improve these students' prospects. "Effective schools" were discovered forty years ago; now we have "effective districts." This story will show that poor, racially isolated districts such as Elizabeth, Orange, Perth Amboy, Vineland, and Union City can sustain dramatic improvements in the literacy of young students, and continue those gains into the middle grades. This progress is something that has not been demonstrated on such a wide scale elsewhere.

The rapid chronology by which young students learn to read and write gives this discussion its sense of urgency. State and nationwide policy debates about improving the quality of classroom teachers or principals are important, but it is not fair to ask parents of today's second graders to wait for these arguments to be resolved before their children are properly educated. We know enough right now about what works in individual classrooms, and we have the evidence that we can accomplish much with the teachers and principals already in place in urban schools. The obligation to tackle classroom practices is a moral obligation, since we are playing with the futures of millions of innocent children.

The obstacles to changing classroom practice are no different in New Jersey than in city school districts in other states, and nothing very new is required to overcome them. We know what to do: *start early, focus on pedagogy* and *show systematic curiosity* about why students struggle, and then *adjust instruction* to meet their individual needs. It looks simple, but is hardly simple to do. It requires changing the work of educators. The culture of education is not conducive to such change, but it can be done. That's the story.

2

EDUCATION IS FOR READERS ONLY

*For the majority of poor children, high quality preschool is unafford-
able or unavailable, so* they arrive in kindergarten . . . less *ready to
learn. When they get there, their classes are larger and their teachers
less qualified than those of wealthier students. They are disproportionately placed in low-ability classes or in the general track; they
therefore take fewer challenging courses and have less expected of
them. In this environment many more poor than well-off students
fail, become disaffected and drop out. If they finish, they are not really
prepared for college; when they go to college, they frequently need
remediation; if they need too much remediation, they never graduate.
Poor urban students may have more family and community problems
than other children, but* their schools have also failed them.
                                    —Jennifer L. Hochschild and Nathan Scovronick,
                                              The American Dream and the Public Schools [1]

When our oldest son was a week away from his first day of kindergarten, his neighborhood friend and mentor, the worldly seven-year-old
Woody, dropped in on our backyard conversation. "Ready for kindergarten,
Ben?" he asked. "Do you know your colors? Can you count to twenty? Do
you know the alphabet?" he pushed. "Because let me tell you, if you get
Mrs. Ames, she'll expect that you know all that stuff!" Woody could have
pressed on: Do your parents read aloud to you? Are there a lot of books in

your house? Do you play with kids who know "all that stuff?" Do you talk to your mom and dad about fire engines and dinosaurs? Are you corrected if you say "ain't"?

This book is about what to do if most kids who show up for kindergarten answer "no" to Woody's questions. There are a few other pertinent questions that Woody would not have asked: Can your parents read English? If not, can they read in their native language? Do you live in a neighborhood where most men go to work? Is your home warm in the winter? And so on.

No reasonable person argues with the assertion that educating students who are very poor and go to school with other very poor children is a lot harder than educating kids who grow up in Woody's neighborhood. The disagreement starts when you try to do something about it.

What Causes the Achievement Gap?

The nation has fiddled around for years seeking the cause of the achievement gap in our schools, coming up with a variety of villains to suit a particular sponsor's ideology, technology, economic interests, or tenured teaching subject. However, there is no great mystery about the cause—children must be able to read, and if they cannot, they cannot be educated. A nonreader cannot succeed at a four-year university (a reasonable definition of a successful public education). An overwhelming proportion of nonreaders are poor black and Latino students. And we know why this is so.

First, black and Latino children are much more likely to grow up in poor families than are white and Asian children. The educational consequences of poverty are magnified when poor children are concentrated in the same schools and districts (and about three-quarters of them are). By 2005, most black and Latino students attended schools where more than 75 percent of their classmates were eligible for free lunch.[2] Racial and social class segregation is worsening.

Second, poor children are much more likely to begin kindergarten without the language, vocabulary, and general knowledge they need to be ready to learn to read. Researchers studying children growing up in professional, working-class, and welfare families have estimated that by age three a welfare-family child has heard 30 million fewer words than a child who picked professionals for his/her parents.[3] Moreover, the words they do hear are much less likely to be words of encouragement or to be used in conversational tones with modifiers and complete sentences. Whereas children in professional families hear positive or encouraging responses six times for every discouraging or prohibiting response, a child in a welfare family hears only one positive reply for every two prohibitions.[4] A comprehensive study of kindergarten students in twenty-three New Jersey city districts found that poor children were seven months behind their peers in academic development, and seventeen months behind in communication ability.[5] Imagine the consequences of starting school at the age of five with the preparation of a three year-old. *This is the gap that is never closed in most city schools.*

Third, poor children are much less likely to be strong readers and writers by the end of third grade, or age nine, a critical threshold. The National Assessment of Education Progress (NAEP) results for nine-year-olds since 1971 document that the gap between black and Latino students and their white and Asian peers has closed discouragingly little over the past twenty years. The NAEP results on the fourth grade test show a narrowing but still very large gap.[6] Between 1992 and 2007, the gap between blacks and whites closed from 32 points to 27 points (scale scores of 203 and 231, respectively, in 2007); the gap between Latinos and whites closed by only one point, from 27 points to 26 points. (See Figures 2.1 and 2.2.) During this time, the number

FIGURE 2.1 TREND IN FOURTH-GRADE NAEP READING AVERAGE SCORES, WHITES AND BLACKS

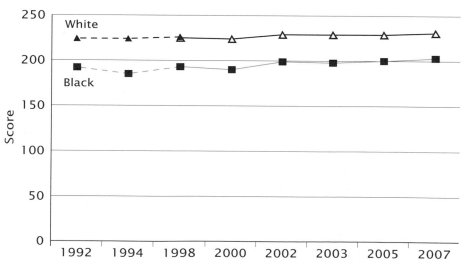

Note: The data for 1998 and onward reflects accommodations for students with special needs.
Source: Jihyun Lee, Wendy S. Grigg, and Patricia L. Donahue, *The Nation's Report Card*: Reading 2007 (Washington, D.C.: National Center for Education Statistics, 2007), Figure 5.

FIGURE 2.2 TREND IN FOURTH-GRADE NAEP READING AVERAGE SCORES,
WHITES AND HISPANICS

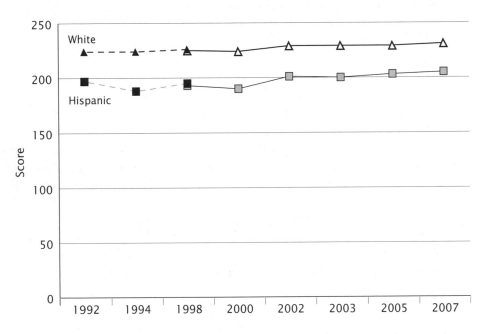

Note: The data for 1998 and onward reflects accommodations for students with special needs.
Source: Jihyun Lee, Wendy S. Grigg, and Patricia L. Donahue, The Nation's Report Card: Reading 2007 (Washington, D.C.: National Center for Education Statistics, 2007), Figure 5.

of poor Latino students more than doubled, making their lack of progress even more troubling.[7]

There is a chronological urgency to learning to read well by the age of nine or ten. Educators are fond of saying that up to third grade is the time to "learn to read"; after that, one "reads to learn." Students who advance to fifth grade reading below grade level have less than a one-in-ten chance of ever reading at grade level. Why? First, the content gets harder. Second, educators know far more about bringing a second grader up to grade level than they do about a fifth or seventh grader. Middle school and high school teachers are not trained as reading teachers but rather see their jobs as teaching increasingly specialized content. Finally, too many students are classified as "disabled" in the middle grades primarily because they are not strong readers. Once classified as such, a bleak academic future is practically guaranteed.

Poverty, stunted language development, and attenuated general knowledge in the preschool years, plus the failure of public schools to produce strong-reading third graders, set the stage for the dismal gap that persists into high school and beyond.

The Achievement Gap Is Stubborn and Wide

Since 1965, the United States has put men on the moon, dramatically increased college enrollment, reduced fatality rates for cancer, eliminated legal segregation, and reduced the inequality between men and women. But the United States has made only halting and marginal progress in closing the achievement gap between black and Latino students and their white and Asian counterparts in elementary and secondary schools.[8]

The persistence and magnitude of the achievement gap are easily documented. Since 1971, NAEP has conducted assessments of students at ages nine, thirteen, and seventeen in reading and math. The results are discouraging: since 1988, no consistent, sustained, or significant progress has been made by black and Latino students in closing the gap with white and Asian students, even though results for white students at ages thirteen and seventeen have not risen.[9] The 2007 NAEP results confirm these trends, leavened only by steady gap-closing results in fourth and eighth grade math.[10] The SAT results over a longer period conform to the NAEP trends, with the same obdurate and yawning black-white gap.

Why Haven't We Done Better?

Since the mid-1960s, there have been a lot of big ideas (remedial instruction, open classrooms, special education, whole school reform, educational television, standards-based instruction, vouchers, charters, and so on). And there have been dozens of self-proclaimed "education" governors, hundreds of commission reports, thousands of conferences, and trillions of dollars spent. But there is no optimism that this gap is going to be closed significantly or soon. While poor minority fourth graders have done a bit better, this progress erodes in the middle grades and disappears by high school (almost a quarter of blacks and more than one-third of Latinos do not finish high school).

While there are plenty of reasons that the national debate about the achievement gap has not produced effective answers, four stand out.

First, we have not been candid or precise about the magnitude and nature of the instructional problems that need to be solved. The work involved is very difficult. Instead of acknowledging the difficulty of grappling with hundreds of individualized problems in each school, we simplify and universalize problems and cast about for formulaic panaceas that ignore the nature of good professional work. Today's students are more likely to be poor, to be from non-English-speaking homes, to be classified as disabled, to be from single-mother families, and to suffer from diabetes and/or obesity than was true twenty or forty years ago. These trends only compound an already challenging job for classroom teachers.

Good instruction is analogous to the practice of good medicine. A good doctor assumes nothing in the absence of a detailed family medical history, results from myriad laboratory tests, and a physical examination. She or he will reference widely accepted quantitative standards for the healthy range for blood pressure, cholesterol, pulse, white cell counts, and so on. Once a condition is diagnosed, the doctor will share with the patient a range of expectations for recovery and the signs that should trigger a revisit for a refined diagnosis and adjusted remedies.

Teachers work in isolation and have none of the direct support provided to doctors by nurses. Their preparation is less rigorous, less relevant, and less collegial. "Student teaching" hardly matches the challenging environment of medical internships and residencies for dealing with practical, everyday problems. The protocols for determining "what's wrong" with individual students are primitive, frequently untested, and not universally accepted. There is no educational equivalent of aspirin for fever or Prozac for depression. And the daily problems frequently change with students arriving and departing, home situations intruding, and administrators demanding more time for non-academic activities.

Seymour Sarason has used medicine as an analogy for teaching to make a different point about the two professions. He notes that public educators are forever promising that they can solve pedagogical problems that have proven so elusive. Scientific medicine on the other hand has never suggested that curing cancer, for example, was a simple or mechanical matter. Sarason writes that the medical community "has made a virtue of its ignorance," not promising to "cure cancers next year or twenty years from now." Instead, medical researchers emphasize the complexities and uncertainties they face in finding cures. "In short," Sarason writes, "scientific medicine said: we will do our best, we will try to learn, but let us not underestimate the obstacles and conundrums we face."[11] Education has rarely owned up to the practical difficulties faced every day.

The medical analogy is not perfect, for doctors benefit from extensive research that challenges conventional treatments, improves diagnosis, unveils new patterns, and so on. Very little education research, on the other hand, is of much help to classroom teachers. In most schools, textbooks determine instruction. Teachers are expected to keep pace and to move ahead, even if all students have not mastered the content. By the time state test results arrive, the school year is over and the results are too general and too late to be of value to anyone. It is like a doctor attempting a cure before the diagnosis has been made.

Second, the adults responsible for doing this difficult work, mainly teachers, have not been well prepared or supported. Policymakers, judges, reformers, academics, and bureaucrats do not bother themselves with the isolation most teachers feel or with the imponderable situations they face daily. Teachers need the time to share war stories and swap suggestions with one another. They need the assistance of supervisors or coaches who recognize good teaching or can offer concrete suggestions to achieve it. They need a clear, specific, and attainable agenda of what needs to be changed, time to implement those changes, and agreement about the measures that will be used to determine progress. They need help to determine why students fall behind, and what might work to help them achieve.

Good teaching is no less arduous than good medicine, just less well compensated. Like medicine, good pedagogy requires clear, quantifiable measures and individual attention based on evidence. A good second grade teacher uses clear and measurable standards to place students on a spectrum of chronological expectations. The teacher should have evidence from assessments that compare her/his students with second graders across the country for vocabulary and reading skills. When these results are combined with district-level assessments and the teacher's own findings, the teacher has the means to individualize instruction by placing students with similar problems in small teaching groups. The teacher needs to take extra time for students who fall behind, even if that means coming in before school, staying late, or using the lunch hour.

This regimen is not easy. Teachers need to be respected for the difficulty of their work. They should be consulted about changes in curriculum and instructional materials. They should be encouraged to spend additional time with struggling students, and compensated for that time. In short, they need to be treated like adults and professionals. Unfortunately, in too many urban districts and schools, such treatment would constitute a profound change in culture and behavior.

Third, we have spent most of our energy, time and money pursuing solutions that ignore the first two conditions. Federal and state policy-makers and bureaucrats think nothing of mandating inconsistent and inconsequential changes that only deflect focus away from classroom instruction. Paperwork and process are the game, not academic achieve-ment. The lowest-performing districts are very practiced at turning out glittering "strategic plans," "progress reports," and "corrective action plans." They have done them for years without detectable progress. Meanwhile, critics decry poor results, all the while piling on countless, irrelevant recommendations and demanding unachievable results. These reformers tend to converse only among themselves, while ignoring those whose work is to be reformed.

Poker is not a perfect analogy for life, although its blend of luck and skill and of rules that must be followed makes it useful enough. In poker, you play the cards you are dealt. Education reformers want a new deal. In fact, most want a different game altogether, one with rules that do not include tenured teachers, weak superintendents, intrusive boards of education, or those pesky children from rural Mexico who cannot read even Spanish, let alone English. Advocates, judges, regulators, and politicians pretend that they are writing on a *tabula rasa*, and that large obstacles such as the differing conditions found from school to school can be ignored.

Effective educators, on the other hand, tend to be "improvers," not "reformers." They play the hand they are dealt, with the players at the table including weak teachers and indifferent leaders. Most importantly, they accept that their responsibility is to educate the students who show up, however far behind they are, and they do so with a sense of urgency.

Most educational policymakers and policies ignore the difficulty and complexity of successfully educating concentrations of poor children. This results in priorities that send educators off pursuing cookie-cutter programs that will not work for most students. Imagine the outcry if a Supreme Court ordered doctors to treat all AIDS patients with a "cock-tail" that favored Merck and Pfizer products. But no one is surprised if teachers are ordered to use a scripted rote system of direct instruction (that does not work). Nor are politicians and voters shy about deciding that recent emmigrants from Guatemala should be exposed to no more than one or two years of instruction in their native Spanish, as they have done in California and Arizona.

Fourth, we have no patience. This is "can do" America, and there is no problem we cannot solve if we just put our minds to it. Is polio stalking a generation? Well, put doctors Salk and Sabin to work on it, and presto, polio is eradicated. If teachers cannot teach kids to read, then introduce the Whiz-bang, Teacher-Neutral, Web-based Reading Program that worked for twenty-eight poor children in Oakland or forty-seven in El Paso. And if last year's fourth graders were lousy on the state reading test, this year's should do a lot better now that Whiz-bang has been ordered.

No Child Left Behind (NCLB) exacerbates this problem. By mandating annual tests in grades three through eight, with no quality controls on either the standards being tested or the tests themselves, the nation is being stampeded to believe that a workable accountability system is finally in place. Worse, NCLB assumes that districts, schools, and commercial packagers have off-the-shelf supplies to produce instant improvements to academic problems that have gone unsolved for forty years.

If only it were so easy, so simple, so packaged. But it is not. Changing classroom practice is an incremental process of starts and re-starts, not a simple matter of following some recipe. We reduce this complex and difficult puzzle to a statistical, bureaucratic, and public relations game, exaggerating scraps of positive news to stave off a searching examination of what needs to be changed.

No part of this explanation for the achievement gap is new or surprising, and none of it should be controversial. In 1966, the Coleman Report confirmed that the variation in achievement could be explained best by two factors: the education and economic level of one's parents, and the socioeconomic class of one's classmates. The third and only other statistically significant explanation—the quality of teaching—frames the obligation of public education to address the deficits created in the first years of life for poor minority students.[12]

A GAP THAT CAN BE SIGNIFICANTLY NARROWED

Despite the ideological warfare waged between Phonics and Whole Language zealots, we now know a lot about how to teach poor children to be literate, even when they are grouped in classes only with other poor minority children. An essential ingredient is not giving up on young children who struggle; another is treating urgently the goal of making all students readers by age nine. The need for both urgency and persistence means that we must devote extra time to students who fall behind—before school, during lunch, after school, even in the summer, if necessary.

These are the characteristics found in "effective schools," and district-wide in a few places such as Union City and Elizabeth, New Jersey, and in the schools operated by the Department of Defense. Of the 100,000 students in the Department of Defense's schools, 40 percent are minority, 50 percent are poor, and the annual *mobility rate is 35 percent.*[13] Despite these challenging conditions, black and Latino students in these schools are the highest performing in the nation, and by a considerable margin.[14] Specifically, the 2007 NAEP reading tests depicted strong results for white students and a narrowing gap for black and Latino students. While nationally, on average, black students scored 27 scale points lower than white students, and Latinos 26 points lower than whites, the respective numbers of students in Department of Defense schools were 17 and 12, respectively. Smaller gaps were found only in states with scattered black and Latino populations, where poverty is not as intense, or where white students scored well below average, as in West Virginia.[15]

Three conditions prevail in Department of Defense schools that contribute to their effectiveness and are not replicated in most city districts. First, while a high percentage of the students in these schools are by definition poor, they are not desperately poor, like students in East St. Louis or Camden are. Second, moderately poor children go to school with solidly middle-class peers. The children of privates are in the same classroom with the children of captains and majors. Third, the parents of all the children in these schools are employed full-time, and are "involuntary volunteers" in the school lives of their children and in the schools themselves. When the Department of Defense sets out "expectations" for parents, they are much more likely to be treated as orders than is true in civilian public schools.

While some may point out that there are other causes of the achievement gap, no reasonable person should quarrel with these explanations. Public schools cannot change many contributing factors, such as parentage or poverty, but they can use the time they have with students to concentrate on literacy, particularly in the first years of school. Early literacy is the essential priority that gets lost or diluted in the swirl of education politics and policymaking.

Since forty years of panaceas have not worked, it's time to try solutions that are simpler to understand but more difficult to implement: practice real pedagogy, and start earlier. While some define pedagogy as the "science" of teaching, it is more a set of habits, practices, evidence collection and analysis, and adjustment and re-adjustment to the learning needs of students. Why push such a basic, unexciting, and obvious solution? Because it works where it is faithfully attempted, and it delivers on the single measure of whether schools succeed: students who are literate enough to self-educate. At the same time, we need to make public education available at age three to children who need extra help to be ready for kindergarten.

Nothing New

The suggestion to concentrate on pedagogy will disappoint those seeking brand-new, techno-driven, or more sweeping remedies. The policies and practices that can work were documented and highlighted decades ago— but like Cinderella, they have been overlooked while commissions and summits have pushed more "systemic," trendy, or dramatic solutions. (Pedagogy's stepsisters enjoy influential patrons.) *By focusing on what works with teachers and students, one opts for less tidy, more perplexing, and more difficult work.* It takes focus, evidence, high expectations, adjustment and re-adjustment, but it does not take anything new.

This book is a story of what happens when a state education department focuses single-mindedly on increasing literacy in the primary grades in its thirty-one poorest and largest school districts. The fact that this is a story about New Jersey hardly limits its application to other states,[16] for the pedagogical problems facing urban districts are similar across the nation, and therein lies this tale's usefulness.

3

The Instructional Problems Facing New Jersey's City Schools Are Mirrored in Cities across the Nation

The New Jersey effort to close the achievement gap in its public schools has contended with some of the same forces that are at play in city districts across the country. While the challenge may be somewhat different from state to state, there are three similarities that are greater than the differences. First, the enactment of No Child Left Behind (NCLB) in January 2002 "nationalized" education policy as never before, with much greater consequences for city districts. Second, cities with concentrations of students from poor families face the identical "kindergarten gap" in the vocabulary, language, and general knowledge of their students and, therefore, the same problems in turning out literate third-graders. In many cities, the problems with closing this gap have been compounded by the recent "Latinization" of urban communities. The failure to concentrate on rescuing struggling primary grade students and devoting whatever time is needed to get them to grade level is both a national habit and a scandal. Third, in city after city, the local boards of education and schools themselves are hampered by a state bureaucracy that mandates adherence to strict rules yet has very little understanding of what works in terms of educating struggling students.

The Impact of No Child Left Behind

To its credit, NCLB turns the spotlight on groups of students who have been overlooked. States must report their test results by subgroups: gender, race, ethnicity, special education and English-language learning status, and eligibility for free or reduced price lunch. Whatever its failings, NCLB has forced public educators to at least acknowledge the needs of students who have been conveniently ignored for too long by too many states and districts. The failure of just one subgroup to make "adequate yearly progress" places a school on a "watch list" in the first year, and then on the "in-need-of-improvement" list thereafter.

By mandating annual standardized testing in reading and math, NCLB narrowed instruction and increased the time devoted to test preparation. Before NCLB, some states used a "high stakes test" to determine eligibility for high school graduation. Tests in the elementary or middle grades were intended to shed light on gaps in teaching and learning and to give "early warning" to students and schools that were falling behind. After NCLB was passed, these types of tests are more frequent and carry significant consequences for underperformance. If a failing school does not improve, the law imposes penalties that can include diverting Title I funds to parent-selected tutors, replacing the principal, transferring teachers, converting to a charter school, or even handing the school over to a private management company.

The results from these tests provide the raw information for the NCLB "accountability" system. NCLB yields an annual scorecard of school performance nationwide that identifies "failed" schools and districts and that receives rapt attention from the media, educators, and politicians. Since NCLB is most influential in districts eligible for Title I funding, NCLB is disproportionately consequential in the city districts that enroll most Title I–eligible students. In fact, there are no federal statutory consequences for underperforming schools that do not receive Title I funds. City districts that have the greatest concentrations of children from poorest families are held to the same expectation as affluent districts. Therefore, a city school that starts off with a large proportion of underprepared students from poor backgrounds can exhibit dramatic progress in improving achievement yet still end up on the "failed schools" list as more stagnant affluent schools escape notice.

Educators "manage what is measured." When they are confronted with standardized tests—the results of which can affect their school budget—the outcome is a constricted curriculum that takes time away from untested subjects such as music, art, and history to concentrate more time on literacy, math, and science. In states with decent standards and with tests that evaluate powerful skills and content, this concentration may not be harmful. But in too many urban districts, the high stakes test environment has focused not on improved instruction, but on drills and preparation that are bloodless and boring to teachers and students alike.

Meanwhile, in affluent districts that receive no Title I funds and where students perform well above the state thresholds, NCLB is an inconvenience on those few days a year when state tests are administered. A curriculum in such a district is much more likely to be driven by what it takes to score 3 or 4 on Advanced Placement tests than by the content of state academic standards or tests.

In the way that it is constructed, NCLB tells us the price of everything but the value of nothing.[1] Had NCLB mandated uniform academic standards and tests across the nation, then it could be used to identify city districts and schools that perform much better than would be predicted given the demographic profile of their students. Instead, there are so many weaknesses and inconsistencies built into the law and its administration that it misleads those who are on a nationwide search for what works.

Using NCLB-approved state tests to identify the states where students perform best, one would be drawn to Mississippi, Texas, and Tennessee, where 87 pecent, 86 percent, and 81 percent, respectively, of fourth-graders achieved proficiency on the state reading test. In fact, no state had a higher proficiency rate than Mississippi. Yet, when students in those states took the National Assessment of Educational Progress (NAEP) reading test in the same year with students across the nation, they scored fiftieth, forty-second, and thirty-ninth· respectively.[2] These and other states have "gamed" the NCLB accountability system to mislead their citizens and to mock the legislative intent of federal law.

NCLB was conceived based on two untested propositions that had been advanced without empirical evidence or much common sense. The first is the incredible assertion that 100 percent of all students will be able to master subject material based on rigorous academic standards that are (theoretically) set to compete with the highest-performing nations such as Singapore and Finland—all by 2014. Not only does the time period set for achieving this impossible standard defy all research and experience in trying to improve complex systems, but also the goal itself is statistically and practically delusional. The second assumption is that NCLB requires that city districts and state departments of education achieve student performance goals that have never been achieved anyplace on a sustained basis. Furthermore, the obligations imposed on state education departments contemplate a reversal of roles that, while desirable, ignores budgetary, organizational, and staffing realities—state departments are underfunded and under-staffed with persons who do not know how to reform low-performing city schools. In the relatively few cases where state departments have intervened, the results have been disappointing.

Gail Sunderman and Gary Orfield studied six large states (not including New Jersey) for NCLB's impact on the operations and responsibilities of state education departments, and they reached this sobering conclusion:

> With a modest and temporary infusion of additional federal funds, the most conservative government in generations suddenly adopted policies that required levels and kinds of educational gains for every group of students within every school that had never been achieved anywhere. The requirements were set down as non-negotiable, and major progress was required under deadlines that did not fit what research has shown to be the preconditions and time required for successful reform. The fact that the law attached very strong sanctions and embarrassing publicity about educational failure for not reaching goals, which many schools and districts soon learned they could not meet, rapidly deepened the conflict over the law.[3]

LATINIZATION IN THE URBAN SCHOOL ENVIRONMENT

In just fifteen years, from 1992 to 2007, Latinos went from comprising 7 percent of all fourth graders taking the NAEP to 19 percent (blacks declined from 17 percent to 16 percent; whites from 73 percent to 58 percent). The increase in Latinos taking the NAEP test was similar for eighth grade.[4] Latinos have surpassed blacks as the nation's majority minority, and their numbers are expected only to grow.

Nationally, Latinization reflects the growth of the Mexican community in the United States, both native-born and immigrant. The most recent U.S. Census estimates that Mexicans represent two-thirds (65.8 percent) of all Latinos.[5] Moreover, partly as a consequence of federal border policy that has diverted entry from El Paso and San Diego, Mexicans are no longer as concentrated in California, Texas, and Illinois, but are found in all states.[6] Mexicans are a minority among Latinos only in the Northeast and Florida, where Caribbean Latinos predominate.

The impact of Latinization on communities includes an increase in the proportion of families that have incomes under the poverty line, do not have legal immigration status, and do not speak English. The growth in migration from poorer rural areas in Mexico, Central America, and the Dominican Republic means that many children (and their parents) come to school without having literacy even in Spanish. As with poor black or white students, this lack of language development and general knowledge produces very difficult pedagogical issues. As Latinos move into previously majority-Anglo areas, their education is likely to be in the hands of professionals with little experience with non-English speakers or Spanish-language fluency.

The debate among educators over English acquisition has been just as divisive and ideological as the Phonics–Whole Language wars. On the one hand are those who assert that building a student's vocabulary and knowledge in his/her first language greatly facilitates the learning of English. The opposing view is that students are always better off if immersed immediately and exclusively in English. Research on the issue is not conclusive and is viewed with suspicion depending on the researcher's presumed ideological proclivities. Some states have resolved these complicated pedagogical arguments with simplistic "English-only" referenda and statutes; others are equally rigid, mandating that language instruction be offered in Spanish or other prevalent languages.

THE PROBLEM OF BUREAUCRACY OVER PEDAGOGY

Almost all city districts operate in a regulatory and bureaucratic environment that is antithetical to good pedagogy.[7] School districts derive their authority from the delegation of state powers that are specified and enumerated in lengthy statutes and lengthier regulations. The operative verbs are "shall" and "must," and exceptions are rarely permitted. One rationale for regulation is that local school boards cannot be trusted to make sensible decisions about the candlepower needed to light classrooms, the qualifications required to teach Advanced Placement physics, or how to observe Violence Awareness Week. Rules have the force of statutes, and their reach is universal. State departments make no effort to distinguish important from trivial regulations, but insist that everything in the code must be honored in a complete and timely manner (no matter that regulations are inconsistent, vague, even idiotic). All the "comprehensive plans" required by the New Jersey education code would level most of Maine's forests (the code itself eats up 1,600 pages).

Camden and Gary, Newark and Los Angeles share these pressures on city schools. But what one can do to improve the chances for poor children in cities is clearly influenced by the state those children live in. So our story turns back to New Jersey.

4

THE *ABBOTT* DECISIONS SET THE STAGE FOR ATTACKING THE ACHIEVEMENT GAP

New Jersey is the national test case for determining if more money produces better education. In rankings of household income, spending per pupil, and teacher salaries, New Jersey is consistently among the top three states. It also demonstrates care about educating children from poor families. Analysis by the Education Trust shows that no other state matches New Jersey's effort to target scarce resources to the poorest districts.[1]

New Jersey's financial commitment to poor districts is a product of twenty decisions by the New Jersey Supreme Court (NJSC) between 1973 and 2006 in *Robinson v. Cahill* and *Abbott v. Burke*. (See Box 4.1, page 24) In its 1990 decision (*"Abbott I"*), the NJSC identified twenty-eight municipalities that qualified for a 1977 urban aid program as the districts to receive NJSC-ordered aid; the legislature subsequently added three districts.[2] In 1997 (*"Abbott IV"*), the NJSC ordered that Abbott districts receive funds sufficient to match the average per pupil spending in the wealthiest districts (*"parity aid"*). A year later (*"Abbott V"*), the NJSC authorized districts to apply for "supplemental funding" if they could document that there were "demonstrable student needs" that could not be met by parity funding. Districts could also apply if they could demonstrate that the range of programs, positions, remedies, and services mandated by *Abbott V* could not be financed by parity aid

23

> ## Box 4.1
> ### The "Abbott" in Abbott v. Burke
> ### and Other Explanations
>
> A *New York Times* editorial called *Abbott v. Burke* the "most significant education case since *Brown v. Board of Education*, the Supreme Court's desegregation ruling nearly 50 years ago."* The case was filed by the Education Law Center in 1981 as a class action in behalf of students residing in poor cities. The ELC sought to contest the constitutionality of a school finance system that gave the least funding to the school districts with the most difficult educational problems. It would take more than seven years to clear the first level of argument in the administrative law court and nine years for the New Jersey Supreme Court to reach its first conclusion. The most recent argument took place in January 2008, about the funding available to construct new schools—it could be *"Abbott XVIII."*
>
> Raymond Abbott is forever associated with this case because the alphabet is used to sort plaintiffs. In 1981, he was an eighth grader in Camden's gritty Veterans Middle School. A Camden rarity, he was the son of two white, married parents, a Presbyterian minister and a teacher. Consistent with the conventional journalistic narratives of city kids, Ray Abbott would spend much of his life living on desperation's edge, doing hard time, fathering children with different mothers, and clinging to hopes of a stable, drug-free life (this profile is drawn from Deborah Yaffe's *Other People's Children: The Battle for Justice and Equality in New Jersey's Schools* [Rutgers University Press, 2007]).
>
> Fred Burke was the New Jersey commissioner of education when the case was filed. A political scientist, Peace Corps administrator, and specialist on Africa, he was recruited by then-governor Brendan Byrne from Rhode Island in 1974, having served as its commissioner of education since 1971. Burke died in 2005.
>
> * "A Truce in New Jersey's School War," *New York Times*, Februrary 9, 2002.

alone. The New Jersey Department of Education (NJDOE) was ordered to issue very quick decisions on supplemental aid applications; and, if denied in whole or part, the administrative and appellate courts were directed to review these applications on an accelerated schedule if appealed by the district.

Except, possibly, for federal court mandates in metro-area desegregation cases, no court has been more sweeping and prescriptive than New Jersey's

Supreme Court in "constitutionalizing" educational practices.[3] Given the tangled and unsatisfactory history of successive waves of "reforms" and "wars" aimed at closing the achievement gap, the specificity and range of the NJSC-mandated remedies in *Abbott V* is breathtaking. Constitutional protection and universal implementation by all Abbott districts were ordered for the following remedies, services, positions, and programs:

- Within fifteen months of the decision, high-quality pre-kindergarten programs must be offered to all three- and four-year-old children residing in Abbott districts.

- The state must bear 100 percent of the costs of making all Abbott schools safe and healthy, eliminate overcrowding, provide additional space for the preschool program, and ensure "adequate" facilities.

- Class sizes must not exceed fifteen in preschool, twenty-one in kindergarten through third grade, twenty-three in fourth and fifth grades, and twenty-three in grades six through twelve.

- Each of approximately three hundred Abbott district elementary schools must adopt a model of Whole School Reform (WSR) approved by the commissioner, with preference for Success for All (SFA), a highly scripted reading program developed at Johns Hopkins.

- Every school must create a school management team with parent, faculty, non-teaching staff, and community representatives to approve WSR models and annual, "zero-based" school budgets.

- Every elementary school is to be provided an "instructional facilitator," a "technology coordinator," and a "media specialist."

- There must be one computer for every five students.

- Each middle school and high school is to employ a "community services coordinator."

- Every school is to hire a "parent liaison."

◆   The commissioner is to defer to Abbott district documentation of addi-
    tional needs governing school security, health and social services not
    readily available in the community, nutritional programs, summer school
    and after-school programs, and anything else that meets the "particular-
    ized" needs of Abbott students.

The NJSC assumption in *Abbott V* and subsequent decisions was that
the constitutionally mandated programs, positions, and services would, if
perfectly implemented, ensure that Abbott students would be as well educated as their middle-class peers. As it turned out, some of the "remedies"
actually retarded progress toward the noble objective of the *Abbott* decision.
Notwithstanding those practical considerations, what was beyond doubt was
that the Abbott remedies would swell district payrolls, increase the purchase
of technology and the use of consultants, and greatly increase state funding
and district spending.

Not surprisingly, NJDOE, the Education Law Center (ELC), and lawyers for the governor's administration quickly—almost exclusively—focused
their attention on one question: Are the NJSC mandates being implemented?
Lost in the process was any sustained attention to improving instruction.

By any reasonable standard, as a consequence, New Jersey city districts
have the resources to narrow the achievement gap. A fascinating story
beyond the scope of this report is the dramatic re-distribution in state revenues to poor school districts as a consequence of *Abbott*.[4] Looking back
from 1997, the year of the NJSC's "parity aid" decision, through 2007, state
aid to the thirty-one Abbott districts increased 75.8 percent, moving from
$8,577 per student to $14,394. Meanwhile, the other 585 districts received
just 38 percent more, less than the inflation rate and not enough to keep up
with their enrollment growth. (See Figure 4.1.) Per student state aid for non-
Abbott districts grew from $2,406 in 1998 to $2,783 in 2007.[5] The proportion of all state aid going to *Abbott* districts increased from 50.6 percent
to 56.5 percent, while their property taxes remained essentially flat. In the
meantime, property taxes were rising in non-*Abbott* districts, contributing to
New Jersey's status as the state with the nation's highest property taxes. Put
another way, of the approximately $2.4 billion in increased school aid spread
over eight years, $1.97 billion went to just thirty-one districts. This is not
politically sustainable arithmetic.

In one of the nation's highest spending states, Abbott districts spend
about 120 percent of the average spent in the state's wealthiest districts.[6]

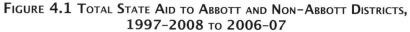

FIGURE 4.1 TOTAL STATE AID TO ABBOTT AND NON–ABBOTT DISTRICTS, 1997–2008 TO 2006–07

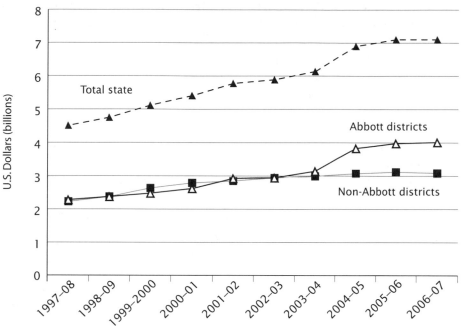

Source: Author calculations from state aid summaries posted by the New Jersey Department of Education on their Web site, at www.state.nj.us/education/data.

When the "parity aid" order was handed down in 1997, Asbury Park was spending $8,268 per student; by 2006 it was spending $21,909, a 165 percent increase. In that same time period, Newark spending went from $9,675 to $16,758, an increase of 74 percent. In the most recent analysis of spending in the nation's one hundred largest school districts, Newark was the highest-spending district by a considerable margin, spending 224 percent of the average of its ninety-nine peers.[7] By contrast, Union City, which plays a central role in this story, saw its spending per pupil increase by 72 percent to $12,431 relying on parity aid alone, placing it in the bottom quintile of the thirty-one Abbott districts for spending.

As long as a request for additional funding included one of the services, positions, or programs mandated or authorized by *Abbott V,* the burden of proof shifted to the NJDOE to reject the request. Abbott districts learned quickly that the fastest path to increased budgets was a request for supplemental funding that was anchored by a finding of

"particularized need" for its students that touched on one or more of
the listed remedies. Particularly in districts with leadership that was
uncertain about how to improve instruction, *Abbott* opened the door
to a bazaar of consultants, packaged instructional programs, "leadership" development, and electronic hardware. In districts such as Asbury
Park, Camden, and Trenton, schools were overwhelmed with programs,
materials, and equipment that was simultaneously introduced, which
produced confusion and uncertain priorities, but no focused attention
to improved instruction.

Districts learned quickly that to build their budgets and payrolls,
they had only to assert "particularized student needs" that could not
be accommodated by generous *Abbott* "parity" aid. They could cite
dubious research about the efficacy of proposed programs and put
the burden on the New Jersey Department of Education (NJDOE) to
disprove both need and effectiveness. In almost all cases, there was
no relationship between the pleadings for more dollars and improved
classroom instruction. In fact, the districts that were most likely to
sue for supplemental funds were those with the least clear vision for
improving instruction. With the state paying up to 90 percent of the
legal bill, there was little incentive not to sue.

Of course, there will always be unmet needs in districts serving
children from very poor neighborhoods. But in high-income, high-tax
New Jersey, the prospects for continuing above-inflation increases in
the poorest districts while raising property taxes everyplace else are
dim. In recent years, the NJSC has recognized the state's deteriorating
fiscal health. In four of the six years between 2002 and 2007, the NJSC
accommodated the petition of successive governors for temporary
relief from full *Abbott* funding, and narrowed the grounds for district
appeals. Meanwhile, legislative opposition to *Abbott* has multiplied,
from a few Republicans in the 1990s to almost all Republicans and
most suburban Democrats today.

(In January 2008, the Corzine administration successfully pushed
enactment of a new school funding formula to replace *Abbott*'s two-tier
funding. The stated intention of the new formula is to fund the more
costly educational needs of poor, disabled, and non-English-speaking
students wherever they live, with state aid that is adjusted for the financial capacity of their local district. With 50 percent of poor children
living outside *Abbott* districts, the administration has a conceptually

appealing case. However, the new law is vague about the transition for those districts for which funding under *Abbott* exceeds the new formula. It appears that they must either increase property taxes dramatically, slash current spending, or a combination of the two. See Epilogue, page 105.)

To summarize: Abbott districts spend at a level that is about 120 percent of that of the wealthiest districts in the nation's highest spending state. The issue is no longer whether school districts with high proportions of poor children receive adequate funding, but whether that funding is used to improve academic achievement.

5

SWITCHING THE PRIORITY FROM COMPLIANCE WITH COURT MANDATES TO PROMOTING EARLY LITERACY

Transitions, particularly when they involve a change in political party, produce the cry for "Change!" Otherwise, what was the campaign fuss all about? Bureaucrats and educators are accustomed to new governors, commissioners of education, or superintendents laying out a new agenda that implicitly criticizes the policies and actions of their predecessors.

The advent of the administration of James McGreevey in 2002 was no different in that it brought major organizational and programmatic changes to *Abbott*. What was different was the level of preparation and consultation at the root of the changes. After his narrow defeat by the incumbent governor, Christine Whitman, in 1997, McGreevey retained his campaign organization, including his adviser on education policy, Lucille Davy. He formed an advisory group of educators who met frequently and reached out to effective education governors, such as Jim Hunt of North Carolina. Davy consulted extensively with the Education Law Center (ELC), the Association for Children, and other *Abbott* advocates on a plan to create a new division within the New Jersey Department of Eduation (NJDOE) that would focus on extending and improving preschool education and on early literacy.[1] ELC was consulted about its choices for commissioner, the assistant commissioner of the new division, and the early childhood education positions.

For commissioner, McGreevey nominated an enterprising and iconoclastic homegrown educator, William Librera. Librera was the former superintendent of Montclair and Bernardsville, where he developed a reputation for tweaking the system's nose and showed openness to new approaches. A student of Mexican history, jazz, and basketball, Librera operated like a combat engineer to clear away the wreckage so that public schools—particularly city schools—could get to the business of educating kids. He happily took on lawyers, the state board of education, even the governor's office, to advance the new *Abbott* agenda. In the pitched, inside warfare that sprung up, Librera was almost always supported by Governor McGreevey.

CHANGING THE FOCUS

The most visible change was the creation of a collaborative relationship between the McGreevey administration and the ELC. At the urging of ELC, McGreevey quickly issued an executive order creating an advisory council that would meet monthly to track issues in *Abbott* implementation. ELC also agreed not to oppose a "timeout" from the New Jersey Supreme Court (NJSC) in the implementation of the many court-ordered remedies and in supplemental funding increases for the 2003 fiscal year. The stated goal of the new collaboration was to use *Abbott*'s generous funding to close the achievement gap. After thirty years of litigation, it was a heady time. Plaintiff and defendant agreed on the objectives and even the leadership of the new Division of Abbott Implementation.

The new division brought together all the *Abbott* activities and programs (except facilities, oversight of which was not transferred to the division until 2006), previously spread across five divisions. Instead of a focus on compliance with judicial mandates, the emphasis shifted to a simply stated criterion of district accountability: Have students mastered the New Jersey Core Curriculum Content Standards? Early literacy, leading to the goal of making every third grader a reader and writer of English, was now the first priority.

The heart of the new division's work rested on the previously cited explanation for the achievement gap, that is, poor children from neighborhoods of concentrated poverty starting kindergarten with large gaps in vocabulary, language, and general knowledge that are never closed.

Given the opportunity to begin working with poor students at age three, and with the generous funding mandated by the NJSC, there was no reason that *Abbott* districts should not significantly narrow that gap by third grade. That was the working premise of the new division, and it was a theme repeated incessantly over the next five years.[2]

To track academic progress closely, the division established a broadly based working group that developed the specifications for a student-level database. Most evaluation is based on annual state test results reported by grade level and school, so that this year's fourth graders are compared to last year's, the method employed to determine if "adequate yearly progress" is made under the No Child Left Behind law. Other methods use small, representative samples of students who are given standard tests (for example, the National Assessment of Educational Progress [NAEP]), or use regression analyses to try to isolate factors contributing to academic progress. None of these approaches are as reliable as following individual students over time while also capturing data on contributing factors such as teacher qualifications and experience, class sizes, special programs, and so on. Soon, the proposed database was recognized as an essential tool for evaluating all students and schools, not just those in Abbott districts, so responsibility for its development was transferred from the Abbott Division to the deputy commissioner.[3]

EVIDENCE SUPPORTED THE CHANGE IN DIRECTION

The new division had more than intuition and research to justify its sharp change in policy and practice: there were several *Abbott* districts that had demonstrated that a focus on improving early literacy could produce impressive performance gains in higher grades. For years, researchers have noted the plateau of improved results that appears to set in at about fifth grade, producing national results that are encouraging on fourth grade tests, begin to fade by the middle grades, and disappear in high school. Having concrete examples of good practice and improved results was essential to diluting the natural skepticism and distrust that accompanies any top-down change. Three districts—Union City, Perth Amboy, and West New York—delivered consistently strong results in densely populated, high-poverty communities where most parents spoke only Spanish at home. They also stood out because the improved results were across the board and not limited to schools led by extraordinary principals.[4]

The highest-performing district with concentrated poverty on the 2001 fourth grade language arts test was West New York (91.3 percent proficiency), followed by Union City (79.3 percent) and Perth Amboy (75.2 percent).[5] What set these districts apart was the coherence of their approach to early literacy, the continuous use of benchmarks and assessments to gauge student needs, the integration of preschool with kindergarten, and the extra time given struggling readers. In short, they practiced pedagogy.

There was one more feature common to West New York, Union City, and Perth Amboy: none had applied for supplemental aid under *Abbott V*, and they spent noticeably less per pupil than the average Abbott district. In 2002, they were 21st, 23d, and 26th, respectively, in per-pupil spending out of 30 districts (in 2006, they ranked 27th, 26th, and 24th, respectively, out of 31 districts). Citation of this fact produced a backlash from the plaintiffs' attorney, the legislative black caucus, and some superintendents of higher-spending, lower-performing districts who inferred that the emphasis on early literacy was a thinly disguised justification for cutting *Abbott* budgets.

THE SUCCESS OF UNION CITY

The more data are analyzed, the more it becomes apparent that Union City was the Abbott district that had established the most cohesive and best-documented approach to improved instruction. In short, its impressive achievement in terms of increased student performance could be explained by the effort it expended. Since the NJDOE new focus on early literacy borrowed so heavily from policies already in use in Union City, a brief description of them is in order.

Union City is the nation's most densely populated municipality and, by the most widely employed measure of poverty—eligibility for the free lunch program—New Jersey's poorest.[6] English is rarely heard on its streets; 96 percent of its students are Latino. An old-fashioned political machine runs the town—the mayor appoints the school board and influences the hiring of just about everyone else. Predominantly Cuban-American in the 1970s, many of Union City's students today are from the Dominican Republic, Mexico, or Ecuador, and often they are poor, and illiterate even in Spanish. Again, Union City is one of the lowest spending Abbott districts ($12,431 per student in 2006, ranking twenty-sixth out of thirty-one).

So why is it that over the past five years, almost 70 percent of Union City's fourth graders were proficient on the state's benchmark fourth grade literacy test, while only half of students with similar characteristics in other districts were passing?[7]

In fact, Union City may be the first urban district in the United States to sustain academic achievement into the middle grades and effectively close the gap between its students and those in non-urban districts. On New Jersey's eighth grade math test in 2006, Union City and non-urban students were proficient at 71.0 percent and 71.6 percent, respectively; for language arts, the comparable numbers were 76.6 percent and 80.6 percent. Between 1999 and 2006, eighth grade students in Union City closed the gap in math with non-Abbott students from 26.3 percentage points to 0.6, and in language arts, they went from 23.3 percentage points behind to only 3.0. Such steady and sustained improvement in the middle grades is somewhere between very rare and nonexistent. (See Figures 5.1 and 5.2.)

FIGURE 5.1 PERCENTAGE OF UNION CITY FOURTH GRADE STUDENTS PROFICIENT OR ADVANCED PROFICIENT IN LANGUAGE ARTS, COMPARED WITH STUDENTS IN ABBOTT AND NON-ABBOTT DISTRICTS, 1999-2007

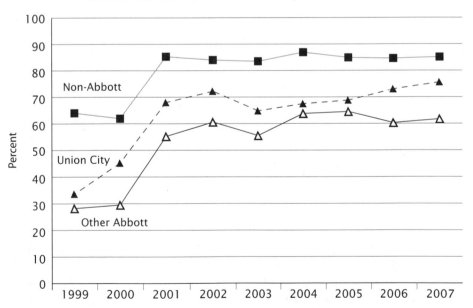

Note: In 2001, the New Jersey Department of Education revised the cut score on the fourth grade Langauge Arts Literacy test, which had the effect of increasing the proficiency percents by about twenty-one points statewide.

Source: Peter Noehrenberg, "Pass Rates by Subgroup 4th Gr. LA '99–06," New Jersey Department of Education Statewide Assessment Data, December 8, updated by author.

Here are the (familiar) ingredients that best explain Union City's consistently better performance:

◆ Union City focuses on academic achievement and uses performance on state and district assessments as its principal accountability measures. It dissects the New Jersey Core Curriculum Content Standards (CCCS) and the state assessments to identify which of hundreds of "progress indicators" are the most powerful and important in rewriting the district curriculum. Union City jettisoned most textbooks, preferring software and instructional materials better tailored to the core standards and state tests. Therefore, everyone involved—teachers, students, parents, and administrators—has a clear idea of what is to be taught and learned.

◆ Union City stresses early literacy. Even before the 1998 Abbott decision that mandated preschool for three- and four-year-olds, Union City worked with community day care programs to increase the exposure of their children to language, Spanish or English, by distributing books in return for at least one "read aloud" session daily. It increased the time devoted to literacy in the elementary grades from thirty minutes for reading and thirty minutes for writing in 1988 to 111 uninterrupted minutes in 1989 and to 120 minutes in 1993, and added even more time for struggling readers. It set up classroom libraries tailored to the needs of each class's students, and constantly measured progress to determine which students needed what extra help. The tie-in between preschool and early literacy produced dramatic results: 83 percent of Union City third graders who had attended preschool in Union City were proficient on the state's 2006 literacy assessment, compared to 73 percent for Union City students who had not attended preschool and to 64 percent in all Abbott districts. The same year, 87 percent of non-Abbott students were proficient—Union City had achieved a nearly complete closing of the achievement gap among students who had attended preschool in Union City. (See Figure 5.1.)

◆ Union City analyzes the probable reasons that students fall behind and *spends whatever time is required* to bring them up to standard. Struggling students are expected to participate in extra sessions during the school day, including during breakfast, lunch, or after school. Students that share similar problems are put in small groups for more intensive instruction during the two-hour daily literacy block.

◆   Union City *continuously measures* the progress of all students through district assessments that are completed every eight weeks. Supervisors work with teachers to diagnose problems and prescribe specific follow-up. So, if 80 percent of all third graders miss question number 17 on a test, the central office knows that it has a district-wide problem; or, it may see that most of the students who missed question number 9 are from just two schools; or, that question number 11 was trouble only for students in fifteen classrooms scattered across town. Its *student database* provides teachers, parents, and principals with timely information on what needs to be stressed with each student.

◆   The Union City school district *enlists teachers* to help solve pedagogical puzzles. Teachers are closely involved in developing the curriculum, in experimenting with new approaches, testing and selecting instructional materials, and adapting technology to facilitate instruction.

◆   Union City sees *literacy as the doorway to deeper and more rigorous learning*. It has *deemphasized textbooks* as the centerpiece of instruction and has opted for a curriculum that is carefully aligned to core standards and state tests. Novels, primary materials, and essays have replaced texts and anthologies. The district emphasizes writing of all kinds (journal, poetry, research papers, short reports, short stories) and develops projects that cut across at least two disciplines (for example, writing a research paper on evolution that uses findings from the *Beagle's* voyage to the Galapagos to touch upon history, biology, geography). Its mathematics curriculum has been constructed in much the same way, leading to dramatic results on state assessments.

◆   Union City knows how to *teach English to immigrant Latinos*. Ninety-two percent of Union City students are Latino; 75 percent come from homes in which only Spanish is spoken. As with general instruction, there is no one program or formula for teaching English-language learners. Age, schooling experience, the literacy level of parents, Spanish vocabulary, and reading ability are all considered in placing students. Some students may breeze through the Spanish-only "port of entry" class in two months; others may linger for a year. Union City offers diverse, age-appropriate literature and nonfiction reading, so that a thirteen-year-old immigrant can read about soccer and not Goldilocks and the Three Bears. It has pioneered using iPods to provide the English versions of texts being read in Spanish.

The Grade Eight Proficiency Assessment for math is a decent measure of how well students are being educated in the middle grades because it requires mastery of writing, vocabulary, and reading comprehension to answer open-ended word problems and explain one's procedures. Figure 5.2 compares Union City's eighth graders to other Abbott districts and to non-Abbott students between 1999 and 2007.

FIGURE 5.2 PERCENTAGE OF EIGHTH GRADE UNION CITY STUDENTS PROFICIENT OR ADVANCED PROFICIENT IN MATH, COMPARED WITH STUDENTS IN ABBOTT AND NON–ABBOTT DISTRICTS, 1999 TO 2007

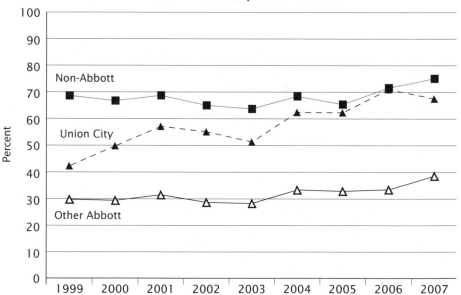

Source: Peter Noehrenberg, New Jersey Department of Education, December 4, 2006, updated by author based on NJDOE statewide data, 1999–2007.

As can be seen, Union City students perform much closer to average New Jersey students than they do to their peers in other Abbott districts.

THE LESSON FROM UNION CITY: WORK SMARTER

Union City's dramatic improvements rely on maintaining the kind of pedagogical culture described above. Doing so requires a commitment by district leadership and middle management to keep the focus on continuous assessment of student work and adjustments to classroom instruction.

In the fall of 2002, the NJDOE recruited Fred Carrigg, the executive director for academic programs in Union City and the principal architect of its thirteen-year campaign of radically improved results, through an "intergovernmental loan" (meaning he would be compensated by the state at his Union City salary, which was considerably above that of the New Jersey Commissioner of Education). At the time, Carrigg had thirty years of experience, beginning as a bilingual teacher and rising to become the supervisor of the Bilingual/English as a Second Language (ESL) programs (an unusual feat for a Trenton Irishman in a heavily Latino city). When Union City's schools, due to poor academic results, were threatened with a state takeover under newly enacted law (its neighbor, Jersey City, was placed in state control in 1988, and remains there as of this writing), the mayor ordered the superintendent to improve the results, or else. In turn, the superintendent gave Carrigg responsibility for all curriculum and instruction and empowered him to do whatever was necessary to dig Union City out of its hole.[8]

Carrigg is an effective educator because he relies on the evidence of student work to make pedagogical decisions and he acts on his belief that all students deserve whatever it takes to get them to succeed academically. Politically savvy and naturally curious, he is well read about what works in improving academic achievement. He also understands the nature of the games played between schools and districts, districts and the state, and the state and the federal government.

What happens when you take habits and practices that Union City built up over a decade and try to introduce them into districts with very different demographics and politics? The next chapter continues the New Jersey story, examining how Union City's lessons work for three-year-olds.

6

PROVIDING QUALITY PRESCHOOL
IS NOT CHILD'S PLAY

The nation is waking up to the efficacy of quality preschool. Thirty-eight states now fund widely varied programs that enroll almost one million children. Standards for teachers, aides, and curriculum are rising. But funding is insecure, quality is inconsistent, and little progress is being made in enrolling more three-year-olds.[1]

New Jersey provides encouraging evidence that we can improve preschool classroom quality on a large scale. In its *Abbott* rulings, the New Jersey Supreme Court (NJSC) drew on a few studies that found that the long-term effects of attending a high-quality preschool were positive and life-long. Even if preschool were not followed by a quality public education, the research demonstrated that its "graduates" were more likely to finish high school, stay in the workforce, get married, and stay out of jail than were their peers who did not go to preschool.[2]

As a consequence of *Abbott V* and *Abbott VI,* no state has done more than New Jersey to deliver on its promise of high-quality preschool for disadvantaged children. It ranks first in funding for preschool, preschool teachers' salaries, and in the enrollment of three-year-olds; twelfth in access for four-year-olds.[3] Each Abbott district must give all three- and four-year-olds the chance to enroll in classrooms with no more than fifteen children, taught by a certified college graduate assisted by

41

a teacher's aide, with a curriculum determined by NJDOE to provide a "well planned, high quality" education. In pursuit of these standards, New Jersey now spends on average more than $12,000 per student each year for the six-hour per day, 180-day academic year (another $4,500 or so goes to the after-school and summer "wrap-around").

It is one thing for a court to order high-quality preschool; it is a very different matter to deliver quality to thousands of classrooms teeming with very small people. New Jersey is the first state to mandate a preschool opportunity for three-year-olds, to order school districts to contract with licensed day care centers willing to meet higher standards, and to pay preschool teachers on the salary scale for K–12 teachers—accomplishing all of this on an accelerated schedule was without precedent. The goal in New Jersey goes far beyond the research results cited by the NJSC: high quality preschool is the foundation to closing the "kindergarten gap," and thus producing literate third graders who can aspire, as high school graduates, to a university education.

The notion of "high quality *instruction*" when applied to rooms of playful three- or four-year-old children can be confusing and misleading. Surely, politicians, bureaucrats, and most educators opine, the pedagogy of preschools with their eager, curious, and non-threatening "students" cannot be all that complicated. After all, they reason, no one expects a three-year-old to be able to read or multiply, so as long as the "teacher" prevents dangerous play, ensures good order, and keeps to the schedule for snacks and naps, preschool will deliver on its promise. In fact, the evidence is very powerful that the *intentional* and *artful* structure of school play by a well-trained early childhood teacher can make a measurable difference in the prospects for children from poor family backgrounds.

The dominant characteristic of a high-quality preschool is that children's capacity to imagine and absorb is never underestimated. They are never talked down to.

It is important to distinguish "poor" from "okay" in high-quality preschool pedagogy. Even untrained observers can spot when a teacher has lost control and chaos reigns. A scholar of national prominence, Ellen Frede of the College of New Jersey, recounted watching in horror as a classroom of four-year-olds climbed out the first-floor window and marched around the building while the teacher yelled helplessly.[4] That was a classroom in which children potentially are harmed by their preschool experience. But preschools that insist that their children mimic the academic work expected of kindergarten or first grade students through frequent focus on worksheets and drills are misreading the implications of developmental research by snuffing out the enthusiasm and curiosity so characteristic of preschool children. So, high quality should not be confused with old fashioned drill work.

The more difficult distinctions are those that involve adult management and intervention with children at play. An "okay" classroom is one where the teacher sees her/his role as that of *manager*. So, if it is time for painting, the manager-teacher will ensure that the children are wearing smocks, that paints and brushes are at hand, and that children participate in the clean up. In other words, he or she will perform the necessary tasks, but perhaps not the sufficient ones. Or, the teacher may see play as a time-filler or "busy work," not as an instructional opportunity. In fact, the teacher may decide to pull children away from play to test them with questions with right/wrong answers, or on numbers or letters. So if a child is building a tower with blocks, the teacher may ask him or her to count the blocks or identify the color of the block with the letter C on it.

In a high-quality classroom, the teacher is artful and scientific, seeking opportunities during play to stretch comparisons for "longer," "fatter," "taller," or "greener." The tower-builder might be asked to count, but, more importantly, to engage with the teacher in speculating how the tower can be constructed to go higher and higher. "What would happen if you used the long blocks at the bottom and shorter blocks on top?" might be the question. Always present, too, is the emphasis on language: complete sentences, modifiers, adding less commonly heard words, finding similarities and differences, sounding out starting letters, listening for rhymes, seeking stories that are read—stories that are imagined by the children and dictated to the teacher, read back, and edited, stories that grow out of events in the classroom or at home or on field trips. All of this intent is better served in a classroom that is rich in materials, toys, books, big books, books in Spanish if appropriate, materials for art, and cups and bottles for "water play."

High quality is more likely to be achieved when teachers are properly prepared in institutions where the work of developmental and cognitive scientists is taken seriously and incorporated into the curriculum. High quality also requires that the pedagogical complexities of teaching very young students be recognized in the salaries paid, a necessity achieved in only a few places.

Strong, Expert, and Focused Leadership

To achieve its goal, New Jersey had to surmount three related and over-lapping obstacles: the dangerously low quality of many day care centers that had signed on to become Abbott preschools, a culture of indifference or ignorance among educators to preschool's potential benefits, and an organizational/bureaucratic tangle among the NJDOE, the districts, and preschool providers within districts. Most importantly, the state had to attract the leadership and intellectual power to carry out the nation's most ambitious investment in the education of very young children. Ellen Frede was recruited to direct the Office of Early Childhood Education in the new Abbott Division. She had been closely involved with the Education Law Center (ELC) in arguing for the mandate for full-day preschool beginning at age three. The ELC and also well-organized preschool advocates pushed strongly for her appointment. In addition to knowing the research about quality preschool, she was clear, direct, and confident in her management style. She reorganized the inherited staff of fifteen professionals and recruited early childhood specialists with backgrounds in math, special education, bilingual education, and professional development. She assumed her responsibilities with a concrete and attainable set of short- and mid-term objectives. What follows is a capsule of the results of her energetic, intelligent, and passionate leadership.

The Struggle for High Quality Is Essential, Complicated, Expensive, and Achievable

Preschool without quality is just high-cost day care. It is not a simple matter of buying colorful alphabetic rugs, supplying age-appropriate toys, and finding two adults to supervise play. Most poor children in the United States already attend day care programs, and have for years, without having improved their preparation for kindergarten. Nor is it enough by itself to increase salaries and attract only college graduates as teachers.

There are reliable tools available to measure the quality of pre-schools. For example, the internationally accepted Early Childhood Environment Rating Scale-Revised (ECERS-R) measures the learning environment of preschool classrooms for teaching style, the use of language, program structure, personal care of children, the presence of printed materials, teaching supplies, play equipment, and the participation of parents.[5] According to the ECERS-R, on a scale of 1 to 7, a program should be 5 or higher if it hopes to close or narrow the pre-kindergarten gap for poor children.

A comprehensive evaluation conducted in 2001 documented the nature and magnitude of the quality problem. The report by Rutgers' Center for Early Education Research found that 21 percent of the sampled classrooms were operating at such a low level of quality that they "might even be harmful to children's development." Another 64 percent of classrooms were of slightly better quality but were "likely to have only small effects on children's school readiness." Only 2 percent were of sufficiently high quality to "prepare New Jersey's poorest young children to start school on a par with their peers."[6] In effect, NJSC-mandated programs might have inflicted affirmative harm on one out of each five participating children!

Think about preschool in these terms: a five-year-old has lived at least 43,800 hours by the day he or she starts kindergarten. To make up for the disadvantages of growing up poor and, increasingly, in non-English speaking homes, a preschool gets less than 2,200 hours spread over two years to make up the gap. Providing a nurturing, warm, and safe environment for that time is not enough—that is what the best day care programs have done for years. These hours must be used to introduce a conscious program of intellectual development that is carried out best by a college-educated teacher with special training in the ways of young children. The best research confirms: preschool programs consistently underestimate the intellectual capacity of three- and four-year-old children; and, effective teachers are those who know how to balance adult suggestions with unfettered free play.[7] How to make these important ideas live in three thousand classrooms was the challenge handed to the New Jersey Department of Education (NJDOE).

THE FIRST OBSTACLE: THE LOW QUALITY OF MANY PRESCHOOL PROGRAMS

The work required to achieve higher-quality preschool can be simply described, but not easily implemented. It sounds so intuitively sensible that it borders on the uninteresting.

In pursuing its objective, the NJDOE had to establish a set of standards for what constituted high-quality preschool education. (Note that the language, objectives, and practices described for preschool mirror closely those used to describe Union City's framework in Chapter 5.)

The essential first step was to adopt clear, specific, achievable yet ambitious academic standards. In response to the *Abbott VI* order (March 2000), the NJDOE published *Early Childhood Program Expectations: Standards of Quality*, a guide that included content for the disciplines included in the Core Curriculum Content Standards (CCCS) for K–12 students. Working through a group of practitioners, superintendents, researchers, and advocates, the new Office of Early Childhood Education began immediately to strengthen the 2000 standards, leading to publication of *Preschool Teaching and Learning Expectations: Standards of Quality* in July 2004.[8]

The second step was to adopt a high-quality curriculum that does not underestimate the intellectual capacity of three- and four-year-olds and that is consistent with the standards in *Preschool Teaching and Learning Expectations*. NJDOE limits districts to a choice of five curricula that reflect varying approaches: Bank Street, Creative Curriculum, Curiosity Corner, Tools of the Mind, and High Scope.

The third step was to assemble the intellectual and organizational resources to create an assessment system that sets baselines and instructional targets, and produces evaluative information that can be used to adjust teacher training and classroom instruction. Early in 2002, the Office of Early Childhood Education formed the Early Learning Improvement Consortium, which included researchers and evaluators from NJDOE, Rutgers, William Paterson State University, New Jersey City University, Montclair State University, and Rowan University. The consortium conducted randomized classroom observations using widely accepted protocols for judging instructional quality. This effort produced an annual scorecard of quality for the state, districts, and preschools. Consortium observers also evaluated instruction in both literacy and math skills. The results were used to adjust professional development for district administrators, master teachers, and classroom teachers.[9]

Working closely with academics, consultants, and district practitioners, the Office of Early Childhood Education also developed a self-assessment protocol for districts to use in observing every preschool class at least annually. "Master teachers" conduct these observations and use the results to create a tailored plan for each teacher to address weaknesses and better implement the district's curriculum.[10]

The fourth step was to evaluate the effects of preschool on students entering kindergarten. To do that, the consortium assessed oral language skills from a random sample of kindergarten students at the beginning of each school year. These assessments found that children who had participated in Abbott preschools improved their skills by one-third of a standard deviation. A more rigorous comparison was initiated in 2005 to isolate the contribution of preschool to better preparing Abbott children for kindergarten.[11]

None of these steps is surprising or very exciting. There is no lurking black box that explains improved quality and the existence of significantly better prepared kindergarteners. All of these characteristics of effective instruction have been known for forty years: challenge and respect students, focus on academics, track evidence of student progress, adjust instruction to individual student needs, give special attention to students who fall behind. How many times can one repeat this framework before the reader drifts off with thoughts of "not again!"

THE RESULTS: HIGHER QUALITY

By 2007, about 78 percent of the universe of 55,000 eligible children was enrolled in preschool: 56 percent in community and for-profit providers, 37 percent in district classrooms, and the balance in Head Start. From 1999 to 2007, the percentage of certified, college-educated teachers climbed from 38 percent to 97 percent. One in seven of all three-year-olds in preschool nationally lives in New Jersey (about 18,000 in 2006).[12]

The Abbott preschool program benefits from steady and continuous evaluation. Reliable "before" information on children's skill levels was in hand before *Abbott V,* and it was followed by annual assessments using consistent standards. This rarely happens in public education. As a consequence, the question of whether a higher-quality preschool can make up the gap between poor and affluent children by kindergarten can be answered: yes, it can, but not quickly.

Six years into Abbott preschool, the results have justified the emphasis on quality. More than one-third (37.5 percent) of the surveyed classrooms in the 2005–06 school year operated with sufficient quality (5+ as measured by ECERS-R) to greatly improve preparation for kindergarten; only 1 percent of classrooms scored below 3. More importantly, the quality gap between district-operated and private programs had been erased.[13] The more detailed assessment of literacy preparation, a test called Supports for Early Literacy Assessment (SELA), showed similar gains. SELA employs a scale like ECERS-R that goes from 1 for low quality to 5 for high. The 2007 study found 76 percent of classrooms providing good to excellent preparation (up from 42 percent in 2003) and less than 1 percent scoring below 2 (down from 12.3 percent). The gains in mathematics instruction, unfortunately, were discouragingly modest.[14]

The National Institute for Early Education Research in 2006 used widely accepted measures in spoken vocabulary, print awareness, and mathematical skills to assess a sample of 1,071 kindergarten students. Students were drawn from 563 classrooms in the fifteen largest Abbott districts, with 72 percent having attended one or both years of the Abbott preschool, and the balance having attended no preschool. On each measure, the preschool graduates were found to perform statistically better at the start and at the end of the kindergarten year. "Statistically significant" does not equal "closing the achievement gap." However, kindergarteners who attended two years of preschool cut the vocabulary gap (vis-à-vis the national average) in half.[15]

In addition to these studies, there is compelling evidence from those districts that track individual students beginning with preschool. For the 46.1 percent of Union City's third graders who had attended at least one year of Union City preschool, their proficiency rate on 2006 state tests *matched* the state average on language arts (82.9 percent versus 82.4 percent) and significantly *exceeded* the state average on math (95.9 percent versus 86.8 percent).[16] West New York reported a higher proficiency rate on language arts (93 percent) among the 18 percent of its third graders who could be tracked back to having attended West New York preschool. (The average proficiency rate for all Abbott districts, including Union City and West New York, incidentally, was just 64.2 percent on the state 2006 third grade literacy test.)

Stop to consider the implications of this information. For years, advocates and reformers have pounced on any evidence that the achievement gap is narrowing or that kids in well-led schools achieve high academic marks even if most kids in the same district are wallowing at low levels. Here are some of the poorest students in New Jersey doing as well or better than the "average" kid in New Jersey (a state whose fourth graders scored higher on the 2007 National Assessment of Educational Progress than students in any state except Massachusetts). While some naysayers will argue that being proficient on these tests is not an assurance of true literacy in English or math, these results indicate surprising success in taking the essential first step toward producing students who can master the content and skills required to succeed at higher grade levels and in four-year universities.

As the quality of preschool continues to improve and the cohort of new teachers recruited for its rapid expansion gains experience, there is strong evidence that the most critical step in narrowing the kindergarten gap can be taken: preparing poor children in poor cities so that they can be ready to learn how to read and write well. This is the essential first step to closing the achievement gap, one that is overlooked by most city districts.

THE SECOND OBSTACLE: AN EDUCATIONAL CULTURE THAT DOES NOT RECOGNIZE THE CRITICAL IMPORTANCE OF PRESCHOOL

Too many—maybe most—educators do not accept that a quality preschool is the foundation for improved literacy and math for poor children. When the mandate for preschool was handed down, no Abbott educators dared to attack the idea publicly. However, prior to *Abbott V*, few districts had included preschool in their efforts to improve achievement. In fact, fewer than 3,300 children (6 percent of eligible students) were served in Abbott district–operated preschools. This is in sharp contrast to another court-ordered reform, full-day kindergarten, which was already being provided to 92.5 percent of Abbott-district kindergarteners.

Here is more anecdotal evidence that Abbott educators did not see preschool as a foundation for improved literacy. At least annually, the author conducted face-to-face meetings with leaders of each of the thirty-one districts to discuss only academics. Early literacy was always the first item on the agenda in more than 120 such gatherings over four years. When pressed about the origins of, and solutions to, the literacy quandary, only four or five superintendents ever offered preschool as a part of their answers. Not surprisingly, those who did led districts that achieved comparatively favorable results.

Moreover, most Abbott district superintendents resented having to contract with any licensed day care center that agreed to meet the new quality standards to participate in the Abbott program. Many expressed the private sentiment that if they had the facilities to operate preschool directly, they would happily cut out community providers. They felt that it was messy dealing with agencies and community organizations that were more a part of the welfare system and that were unaccustomed to the closer scrutiny that came with the Abbott rules. Of course, the NJSC mandate was intended to jump-start preschool opportunities, from accommodating hundreds of children in 1998 to tens of thousands just a few years later. If the state was going to make good on the promise of Abbott preschools, there was no time to lose. By 2002, there were 450 providers at 520 sites under contract to 26 Abbott districts, supplying 1,800 classrooms for 27,000 children.

Many day care providers participating in the Abbott program were small family businesses with only two or three classrooms; a few were well-financed and managed community organizations with high academic standards. Some had powerful political connections. Head Start programs, which were singled out by the NJSC for inclusion, operated with a different culture, one that emphasized parental participation and control of the board of trustees, social and health services, and lower standards for teachers and classroom size. All this variety and the fact that most preschools were run by people without recognized certifications or academic preparation, collided with the orderly, hierarchal public school culture.

In short, already-embattled city superintendents had to contend with the confusion of incorporating independent community organizations into the district's instructional program. The absence of direct control added to the resentment about having to include them in the first place and provided a convenient excuse for the organizational and quality problems that emerged.

The attitude of most superintendents reflected early childhood education's stepchild status in public education. Within most university schools of education, which often already suffer from an inferiority complex, early childhood education tends to receive the least respect and resources.[17] For years, there was little science associated with early childhood education, and professors preparing teachers for essentially minimum wage jobs had none of the prestige that went to "educational leadership" degrees. Despite dramatic breakthroughs in neurological and developmental research that demonstrate the phenomenal, sponge-like capacity of young children's minds and the importance of quality inter-action with adults, the educational community has largely ignored its implications. Then-governor Christine Todd Whitman may have spoken for a lot of city educators when she dismissed the NJSC mandate, noting, "Three and four year-olds should be doing what they do best: playing, not cramming for kindergarten."[18]

THE THIRD OBSTACLE: ORGANIZATIONAL BUREAUCRACY

Consider that in 1998 the appropriation for Abbott preschool was zero; six years later, it would approach $500,000,000 and enroll almost 40,000 students. Of these, about 63 percent would be in community or Head Start locations in 1,700 classrooms, the others in district-run classrooms.

In 1998, most Abbott districts had no management expertise in preschool education, and little connection with licensed day care centers that were shortly to become contracted providers. Moreover, most districts had no experience in overseeing large-scale contractual instruc-tional services, and they had inadequate accounting and budgeting talent and systems. Almost two-thirds of all preschool teachers lacked a college degree; many had no more than a high school diploma. Salaries were low and benefits skimpy. So, neither the districts nor the day care centers signing up for Abbott funds and tougher standards were prepared for the changes thrust upon them.

NJDOE had to set enforceable academic standards, organize and implement a comprehensive budgeting system, and assist districts to build the organizational capacity to manage a fast-growing program. Having a leader like Ellen Frede gave the new Abbott Division an unusual advan-tage: a leader who brought expert knowledge and value-added advice to school districts that normally saw the department as an overseer run by underpaid bureaucrats who delighted in playing a "gotcha" game.

There was no audit program in place in 2002 to determine if pro-viders were fulfilling their contractual obligations for balanced budgets, adequate insurance, facility safety and conditions, and personnel. By the spring of that year, the Abbott Division had initiated audits in the three largest districts—Newark, Jersey City, and Paterson—that accounted for about one-third of all providers then under contract. Early audits focused on providers that the districts had identified as being consistently cash-short, or about whom vendors or employees had complained of slow payment. The first audit uncovered a two-classroom family business that was leasing two automobiles from the family's own limousine service, had purchased a tow truck, and listed many casino-related expenses in Atlantic City.[19] By 2003, the Abbott Division had contracted with accountancies for audits of all providers in all districts.

As budget and audit problems mounted, the Office of Early Childhood Education required districts to hire one "fiscal specialist" for every eight contracted providers. The purpose was to build the provider's budgeting and accounting capacity and to permit districts to monitor expenditures more closely. The Office required quarterly reports and sent warnings to providers who did not or could not supply them, or whose reports showed unapproved spending. If the pattern persisted, the district was encouraged not to renew their contracts. In egregious cases or in instances where safety issues remained uncorrected, contracts were halted in midyear. By 2006, about one hundred of the original providers had dropped out or been terminated.

To deal with the organizational and quality issues that accompanied large numbers of small preschool providers, the NJDOE adopted a regulation requiring that any newly contracted provider must provide a minimum of six classrooms.[20] The combination of this rule with the attrition of so many small providers has improved the overall efficiency of preschool for districts and for the NJDOE.

The preschool program had been launched in an atmosphere of distrust and continuous litigation. The ELC and many advocates doubted the commitment of the Whitman-DiFrancesco administrations,[21] with the result that every major policy decision was subject to almost instant litigation. However, Ellen Frede was the choice of many to run the Office of Early Childhood Education; she had worked closely with the ELC and preschool advocates, and had set up collaborative working groups to reach policy consensus, so her group carried out its work in relative serenity. (The truce with ELC did not endure nearly as well when K–12 and facility issues were at stake.)[22]

In the 2007 reorganization of the NJDOE, the Office of Early Childhood Education was elevated to divisional status, and its director,

Dr. Jacqueline Jones, was made an assistant commissioner.[23] The new division was given responsibility for what is traditionally considered "early childhood education," which concentrates on the years from birth to age nine or third grade.[24] This move makes organizational and programmatic sense. A new school aid formula enacted in January 2008 that extended Abbott preschool standards to another eighty-six districts greatly expanded the new division's responsibilities. The 2008–09 school year was designated a "planning" year, during which time the new division was to provide guidance on the expanded instructional, administrative, and financial obligations for each district. However, despite a tripling in the division's workload, it was denied any new staff or funds to carry out its responsibilities. This failure to invest in additional staff will increase the risks that districts newly obligated to provide preschool will fail to meet the quality threshold that makes preschool pay off for poor children.

New Jersey's Judicial Mandates versus the Drive to Improve Classroom Instruction

The drive to make every third grader literate quickly ran into an unpleasant fact: some of the judgments by the New Jersey Supreme Court (NJSC) about what must be done in schools and classrooms to improve academic achievement in the early grades were wrong—seriously wrong. The main culprit was something called Whole School Reform (WSR)—a concept that sought the top-to-bottom scrubbing of schools in an attempt to improve performance.

In *Abbott V*, the NJSC embraced WSR effusively, and made it clear that it expected every Abbott elementary school to do the same. Its decision read:

> Because the evidence in support of the success of whole-school reform encompassing SFA [Success for All] is impressive, we adopt Judge King's recommendation "that the State require the Abbott districts to adopt some version of a proven, effective whole school design with SFA-Roots and Wings as the presumptive elementary school model."[1]

In issuing its mandate, the NJSC relied on the state's expert witness, Dr. Robert Slavin, who was the founder and chief marketer of SFA, and, also, the author of much of the research that was cited in establishing the efficacy of SFA. All Abbott elementary schools were directed to implement SFA or another approved model within three years, and NJDOE was ordered to provide assistance and financial support to make it happen.[2]

In 2002, most New Jersey city districts were not focused on new academic standards or improved teaching, because they were in the fourth full year of responding to the sweeping mandates of *Abbott V.* They were busy establishing school management councils and adopting Whole School Reform models.

By 2002, the efforts by the New Jersey Department of Education (NJDOE) to ensure uniformity in the implementation of the *Abbott V* mandates were taking hold. So in most districts, schools had become the center of attention as new "school management teams" wrestled with WSR models, contracts, and school budgets. Abbott districts were under the gun to ensure that each of the three hundred elementary schools had adopted an approved model of WSR as ordered by the NJSC and NJDOE regulations.

The mandate for WSR adoption reflected a weary and distrustful NJSC. Beginning in 1970, the NJSC presided over two historic school finance cases, *Robinson v. Cahill* and *Abbott*. The first nine decisions in the two cases aimed to correct the inequities created by New Jersey's heavy reliance on property taxes to finance public schools. The notoriously activist court ordered the closing of all public schools in July 1976, ruling that the state had not properly enacted the school finance reform measures that were ordered in *Robinson v. Cahill* in 1973. Faced with the prospect of a chaotic September, the New Jersey State Legislature returned to its un-air-conditioned chambers and enacted a state income tax to comply with the school financing requirement.

By 1990, however, the Court introduced educational questions to accompany those around fiscal equity: What does a constitutional education look like, and how would the necessary educational programs be implemented and supervised by NJDOE? Successive education commissioners in the James Florio and Christine Todd Whitman administrations pointedly ignored the NJSC requests. Tired of waiting, the court ordered accelerated hearings in 1997, at which the education commissioner and the Education Law Center (ELC) presented their answers to a court-designated special master. Both agreed that preschool was essential, although the commissioner sought to limit it to half-days for four-year-olds while the plaintiffs' attorney sought full-day sessions for three- and four-year-olds. Both agreed to full-day kindergarten and reduced class size in the primary grades. The commissioner emphasized early literacy and mathematics, asserting that SFA was the most effective vehicle in elementary schools. The plaintiffs opposed WSR in general, and SFA in particular, seeking instead the establishment of all-day "family and community schools" that would implement the educational practices found in the wealthiest suburbs, with comprehensive social, nutritional, health, and after-school programs added to deal with the problems of poor families ("supplemental programs").

The special master, Alan Odden of the University of Wisconsin-Madison, sided with the ELC on two years of preschool and with the commissioner on SFA to achieve early literacy, but incorporated some of the plaintiff's non-instructional services and positions to fashion an "enhanced New Jersey" SFA model. Both parties accepted the recently adopted New Jersey Core Curriculum Content Standards as the measure of educational effectiveness. The court adopted the special master's report establishing SFA as the "presumptive" model, but permitted the commissioner to add other "research-based" national models. The court cited early literacy as the rationale for its WSR mandate: "The emphasis on reading, writing and communication espoused by [SFA] . . . is the *quintessential foundation for all future gains.*"[3]

The court acted just as the WSR movement was cresting. Begun as an outgrowth of President George H. W. Bush's Goals 2000 effort, WSR was fostered by New American Schools, an organization founded in 1991 by business leaders and former New Jersey governor Tom Kean. New American Schools conducted a competition for new ideas to create schools that would "break the mold," that would teach to international academic standards, and that assumed that "the schools we have inherited did not exist."[4] Like most reformers, the people involved with New American Schools were looking to start with a completely clean slate. With only $50 million to invest in the winning models, it selected eleven from the 686 proposals it received, including four that would end up on the education commissioner's list of approved WSR models.

Even as the idea of a school-by-school strategy gathered steam, by the time the NJSC acted, there was no compelling evidence that WSR in general, or SFA in particular, improved learning. All the research available in 1997 had to do either with how thoroughly WSR models had been implemented, or had been conducted by the WSR vendor or related parties, and therefore was not considered reliable.[5]

By pushing WSR as the best path to improved literacy, the educa-tion commissioner and NJSC were tacitly accepting the premise of the reform movement: city school districts are too corrupt, bureaucratic, or incompetent, or a mix of all three, to assume academic leadership. The court hammered the theme of school-driven reform: "We sense from the evidence . . . that there has long been too little State involve-ment at the school level and too much reliance on remote control through the districts."[6] NJDOE responded with regulations that cut out the district leadership on WSR adoption and school-based bud-gets. In fact, the NJDOE budget software prevented any district mod-ification to the school budgets once the school management teams and NJDOE approved those budgets. Districts were thereby shut out from influencing about three-quarters of their operating budgets.

The mandate for universal adoption of WSR compromised one of the foundations of the school improvement movement: reform should be voluntary and overwhelmingly accepted by a school's fac-ulty. Otherwise, reasoned its proponents, WSR would be just another program crammed down the throats of unwilling teachers. The rules for implementing WSR allowed school faculty to vote on which model of reform they would adopt. SFA, for example, required that at least 80 percent of teachers vote for its adoption; the NJDOE regu-lations specified 70 percent. However, if a faculty could not produce a super-majority to choose a model, then SFA would be imposed on the school. In her survey of teachers over three years, Bari Anhalt Erlichson and her colleagues found that less than half the teachers agreed with the statement: "I felt that my opinion was incorporated into the decision of which model was chosen."[7] If WSR was ever a good idea, its implementation in New Jersey obliterated an essential premise.

MANDATED WHOLE SCHOOL REFORM
EMERGES AS THE BATTLEGROUND ISSUE

By September 2002, all three hundred Abbott elementary schools were supposed to be in at least their second full year of operating with an ap-proved WSR model. (See Box 7.1.) It was soon evident that the process mandated by the NJSC conflicted directly with its concurrent emphasis on early literacy:

BOX 7.1
THE PERFECT MODEL OF WHOLE SCHOOL REFORM AS ENVISIONED BY THE NEW JERSEY SUPREME COURT AND THE DEPARTMENT OF EDUCATION, 1998 TO 2002

As the principal of an Abbott elementary school in one of the larger cities, the first thing you learn is that you must modify the way you run your school. In addition to reporting to an assistant superintendent downtown, you will now also report to a newly formed School Management Team (SMT).

In setting up the SMT, you will receive help from a newly hired "School Reform and Improvement" specialist from the New Jersey Department of Education, who will be available from time to time. You will hold three separate elections to organize the SMT—teachers will vote separately for teacher members; non-instructional staff will vote for staff members; and, all parents will be invited to select representative members. You will be the chair of the SMT and responsible for selecting a community representative after soliciting nominations from parents, teachers, and others. You must document and certify everything. All meetings of the SMT must be advertised and public.

Next, you must form a committee of the SMT to investigate Whole School Reform models and adopt one within two years (your district will set the deadline). There are eight models on the education commissioner's "approved" list that you can choose without having to do extensive research. The committee must document what it did to investigate competing models and make a recommendation to the SMT. To be adopted, 70 percent of all teachers must vote "yes."

After you have adopted a model, you must implement it. Let's say your SMT agreed to choose Success for All (SFA). You start by naming one teacher as the SFA facilitator. This could be one of your effective veterans, who is respected and can work with newer faculty; or, you may want to use the opportunity to get a particularly bad teacher out of the classroom. After the facilitator returns from his orientation, there will be four days of summer professional development to introduce SFA to all affected teachers and coaches. The first change everyone notices is that the familiar basal reading series is out. Teachers will have to learn

(Cont. on next page)

an entirely new system based on "direct instruction," which means a highly scripted, minute-by-minute lesson plan every morning for ninety minutes, accompanied by drills in unison with clapping. SFA uses only its own instructional materials (so no outside books) and permits no teacher-determined variations to the scripted lessons.

When a teacher transfers in the middle of the year from another elementary school that adopted a different model, she must acquaint herself with a brand new system of instruction (aided by the facilitator). Students who transfer from other schools are confused and frustrated by the radically different instruction and content. All the change will be worth it if your students perform well on the upcoming state tests in language arts. Unhappily, the results are disappointing, primarily because most students did poorly on the writing sections, which are half the score. SFA is a reading program that did not include writing.

♦ WSR was untested as an effective instrument for teaching math and literacy. While some models, such as SFA and Expeditionary Learning, were promising, not one was proven. No other state had employed WSR on the scale contemplated by New Jersey. The appropriate test was not if WSR worked sometimes in schools led by effective principals, but if it worked enough of the time under normal circumstances to justify its adoption as a universal mandate. In 1998, WSR failed this test (as it would today).

♦ The NJSC and NJDOE schedule for implementation was rushed, ignoring the reflective nature of pedagogy and the philosophies of most models. Instead of a deliberate process of extensive investigation of various models, and a period of careful implementation, districts were forced to get all schools on board within two years. Every school in Erlichson's studies mentioned the lack of time to plan, train teachers, and absorb the training to adjust teaching. [8]

♦ The WSR mandate turned the public school hierarchy upside down. Schools became the center of not only WSR implementation, but also of budget-making. NJDOE now had to deal with the thirty Abbott districts on preschool, facilities, and annual budgets, in addition to managing annual budget decisions for over 450 schools. The district was shut out. WSR vendors frequently took the place of curriculum and instructional supervisors in the central office. The idea of a coherent district instructional focus went out the window.

◆ While the special master saw WSR as the way to improve early literacy and math, most of the models that were approved by the education commissioner provided no concrete assistance with either. Only SFA and America's Choice offered both. The other models were designed to inculcate higher expectations for students or a more collegial school culture, to introduce computer-assisted instruction, or to ameliorate social and health problems.

◆ Particularly in larger districts, the adoption of different WSR models created an incoherent patchwork of school missions, instructional practice, and curriculum. Newark was typical. By the 2001–02 school year, its seventy-five schools had adopted ten different models. With high rates of intra-district mobility, students or teachers transferring from an SFA to a school that had selected the Comer model would encounter a radically different instructional regimen. There were no district-wide instructional benchmarks and assessments to set objectives or to diagnose literacy problems. Nor was there a coherent reading philosophy. The fact that SFA was not aligned to New Jersey's core standards and assessments showed up in the consistently low performance of SFA schools (not one SFA school in Newark exceeded the Abbott average; not one higher-performing Newark school adopted SFA).[9]

◆ Most of the approved models made no provision for the particular difficulties of educating special education students and English learners, who together were about one-third of all Abbott students. This only reenforced the practice of most districts: isolating these students from their "regular" peers.

◆ The WSR vendors were of very mixed quality when it came to assisting their client schools. SFA had the deepest experience and the most complete program of professional development. Most other models lacked seasoned staff. Districts complained of high costs, poor service, high turnover among the field staff, and inconsistent or irrelevant advice.

◆ Most districts were mere observers of the selection of WSR models. Some superintendents were actually relieved by the NJSC mandate, because it obscured their responsibilities to solve difficult pedagogical problems. They handled the paperwork and compliance games masterfully; they could blame poor results on the court mandates. In their 2001 study of fifty-seven Abbott schools in nine districts, Erlichson and Goertz concluded that "the Abbott regulations created considerable ambiguity about the role of district administrations in the WSR . . . process," and "districts have turned much of their reform efforts to the various developers working within the district." Erlichson quotes one principal: "'It is no longer that the directors downtown have anything to say to us in regard to curriculum. The developers have taken over.'"[10] A few districts—West New York, Union City, Perth Amboy—technically complied with the WSR mandate by adopting the least intrusive and totally non-instructional Comer model in each school, while retaining the district's control of curriculum.

◆ For many school and district leaders, WSR adoption had little to do with improved literacy practices and everything to do with increased budgets and payrolls. The court's "enhanced" SFA model encouraged this outlook by adding several positions to SFA's basic design. To be sure, some staffing increases reflected the mandate to reduce class sizes to no more than twenty-one in K–3, twenty-three in fourth through sixth grades, and twenty-four in seventh through twelfth grades, and some were a result of increased enrollment. Overall, the number of teachers in the Abbott districts increased by 21 percent in the five years following *Abbott V,* while enrollments rose by just 3 percent. In Asbury Park, the faculty increased by 19.2 percent even though enrollment declined by 13.9 percent; in Jersey City, the number of certified teachers increased by 24.3 percent, while enrollment went down 4.6 percent.[11]

Abbott offers a very powerful lesson: courts can and should influence issues of funding equity; they should absolutely avoid using their authority to mandate how education is practiced.

8

DISTRICTS MUST LEAD IF ACADEMIC PERFORMANCE IS TO IMPROVE

By 2002, city schools and districts were under the gun to sort through a tangle of new requirements from the New Jersey Supreme Court (NJSC) and the New Jersey Department of Education (NJDOE). The goal of producing literate third graders went on the list with everything else. The character and magnitude of the effort that district leadership would need to put forth to realize the literacy goals, however, were inconsistent with the *Abbott V* and NJDOE mandates. The lawyers, justices, and NJDOE officials stressed implementation of dozens of *Abbott* "remedies," most of which had little to do with improved classroom instruction.

There is a limit to how much top-down change can be imposed, which is why so much educational "change" ends up as only a hierarchal paperwork exchange. Consider what a typical K–8 Abbott school faced in just the period from 1996 to 2002:

◆ New Jersey introduced its Core Curriculum Content Standards (CCCS) in 1996 for literacy, math, science, and six other subjects, and announced that math and literacy tests would be given in 1999 in grades four and eight. Assuming that schools would turn first to what was to be tested, a K–8 school would need to discern which were the most important "progress indicators" from literally hundreds in each subject, since trying to teach all of them was impossible. NJDOE refused to distinguish its "power" standards from those that are less important and less likely to be tested.[1] It would be up to each school or its district to figure out what cumulative math skills and content would have to be taught in fifth through seventh grades, so that eighth graders would have a fighting chance. The non-Abbott districts quickly learned that eighth grade math standards were built on the conceptual foundations laid in fifth and subsequent grades. As late as 2002, however, most Abbott districts were using math textbooks that were not aligned to the math standards adopted in 1996.

◆   As all schools were preparing for the spring 1999 tests, NJDOE issued regulations mandating that every Abbott school create a School Management Team (SMT) of teachers, non-instructional staff, and community and parent representatives. The regulations outlined very prescriptive procedures (such as how widely the principal must search for community representatives, and what evidence of the search must be reported in the operating plan).

◆   In the 1999–2000 school year, each Abbott elementary SMT was to begin selecting and installing a Whole School Reform (WSR) model using the NJDOE-prescribed process.

◆   The same year, the budgeting process was turned upside-down, with each Abbott school now responsible for building a "zero-based" budget that was subject to detailed NJDOE review and approval, but with no role for the district headquarters.

◆   NJDOE administered the first fourth grade assessments in 1999, with little preview of what content would be tested and how it would be tested. The results for most Abbott schools were, predictably, discouraging.[2]

◆   Abbott schools were required to enter a WSR contract with an approved vendor by the end of the 2000–01 school year and report on implementation in the fiscal year 2002 budget request.

◆ On top of all this, No Child Left Behind (NCLB) came along in 2002, with a new set of requirements that used state test results sorted by ten subgroups to determine how Title I funds could be used in each school.

This is an awful lot of change in just six years for an institution— public education—that has proven more resistant to change than even the Marine Corps or the Roman Catholic Church. The policies may have changed, but in most city districts, these statutory and court-ordered mandates yielded few visible changes in classrooms. Most districts, for example, did not revise their curricula to reflect the new curriculum standards, but rather continued with the same basal reading series and math textbooks that were adopted in the 1980s or 1990s. Even with disappointingly low state test scores and more severe consequences for low performance with the advent of NCLB, most districts proceeded as if they could improve results without changing what and how students were taught.

URBAN DISTRICTS NOT FOCUSING ON THEIR PEDAGOGICAL PROBLEMS

If the goal of state policy is to improve instruction, one must operate with a realistic profile of the leadership, competency, and culture in target districts. Generalization is dangerous when extended across 31 school districts, 460 schools, 320,000 students, and thousands of educators. It can be assumed, but not asserted, that the description below of New Jersey urban districts would hold up in most cities. Indeed, much of what follows is not limited to cities, but characterizes public education generally:

◆ *A culture that prizes process and paperwork over solving instructional problems.* District personnel are masters of the kind of reporting called for in the boxed, hypothetical NJDOE *Abbott X* orders. They grumble about bureaucracy, but produce the mandated paperwork, while changing nothing in classroom practice. Most Abbott districts have produced beautifully detailed and comprehensive plans for federal and state agencies for a decade without detectable improvement in practice or results. This is what passes for "accountability" in most instances.

◆ *A lack of systematic curiosity about why students are not learning.* The absence of an updated and clear curriculum, for example, makes it impossible to determine where students are failing, simply because they are not being taught what was tested. The near-total absence of interim benchmarks and district tests leaves only state test results to flag problem areas. But New Jersey supplies such generalized information on its test results so late in the academic year that it is useless to educators and parents (Massachusetts, on the other hand, provides the answers to every test question so that its educators can see patterns of mastery or difficulty).

◆ *Isolated teachers who are given little advice and support by those who supervise them.* Principals often act as managers and disciplinarians, not as educators working collaboratively with their faculties to improve instruction. Many central office staff visit classrooms only rarely to observe teaching and learning and, when they do, they have little capacity to suggest constructive changes.

◆ *A headquarters that lacks the knowledge and competencies to solve increasingly difficult issues, such as rising special education classification rates and Latinization.* Few districts collect and analyze essential information on classroom performance to draw conclusions or hypotheses. There is ample evidence that many urban districts are segregating and neglecting the educational needs of special education and Latino students. Abbott districts classified students as "disabled" 20 percent more than non-Abbott districts did, and the rate went up as the content increased in difficulty. Whereas "only" 15 percent of fourth graders were classified that way in 2006, almost 20 percent of eighth graders were.[3] Too often, districts did not expect their disabled and English-learning students to master the state curricular standards; instead, they and their teachers were given "lite" instructional materials.

◆ *A political and professional environment that seeks mechanical or formulaic answers to very complex instructional problems.* For forty years, teachers have been subjected to successive waves of "silver bullets." The public thinks that the instructional process is simple, and that if there is a problem, the solution is also simple: tweak the number of minutes here or add a software package there and, voila, success!

The story in Box 8.1 (see page 68) raises the central question of this report: Can a state education department do anything to help that composite teacher? The mismatch in scale suggests not: there are about five thousand Abbott teachers in the primary grades, and the NJDOE early literacy staff never exceeded fifteen professionals. Despite this mismatch, the answer is "yes," a state education department can help solve pedagogical puzzles in poor districts. All it needs to do so is to focus relentlessly on academic achievement; use analytical data on student achievement to guide its work; attract experienced and effective educators who work with evidence and questions, not The Answer; adjust to local conditions; and, gain access to districts, schools, and classrooms. And yes, adequate funding is necessary.

Simplicity and focus are essential to changing classroom practice. To cut through the clutter and the numerous and frequently inconsistent mandates, policies, reporting dates, corrective action and strategic plans requires a relentless effort to shift the conversation and effort to producing literate students.

Making the Message Consistent

Repetition works. Miller Lite: tastes great, less filling. At Ford, quality is job one. At the Abbott Division, the message was equally repetitive: "Every third grader needs to read and write well. The path to this goal is high quality preschool and intensive early literacy in grades K–3. Nothing else counts as much." Every document the division issued for five years emphasized the need to focus on preschool and primary grade students. At least annually, the division held a face-to-face meeting with the leaders of each district to discuss academic performance, and in each meeting, early literacy was the first item. Where results were poor, the division offered the assistance of the Office of Urban Literacy.

NJDOE erased the inconsistencies between federal and state reading programs. Reading First, the federal initiative to improve early literacy, provides substantial additional funding for districts whose applications were approved by state and federal departments of education. New Jersey adopted identical guidelines for Reading First and Abbott, which meant

---

BOX 8.1
A TYPICAL STORY

A veteran fourth grade teacher works in a predominantly African-American school in a poor neighborhood. For ten years, she and her colleagues have faithfully taught from a commercial reading series adopted by the district. On the state's fourth grade language arts test, no more than 60 percent of her students have ever achieved proficiency.

Recently, two newly arrived Mexican immigrants joined her class. Both students are from rural Mexico, with spotty primary school attendance there, and neither can speak any English. The teacher does not speak Spanish, and there is no bilingual program in her school. Her colleagues face the same situation, and all they can think of is to place the new students in the lowest reading group and try to build some vocabulary by pointing to common objects ("pencil," "book," "map"). The new students try, but are lost. Already facing a challenging situation, the teacher is seeing the problems compounded, and has nowhere to turn.

---

that the U.S. Department of Education agreed to use its funds on classroom libraries (a favorite of the reviled Whole Language movement) and supported native-language instruction (against its "English-only" inclinations). So, too, were the Abbott literacy standards consistent with what districts and schools had to do to improve performance in schools that failed to make "adequate yearly progress" (AYP) under No Child Left Behind.

LOOSENING OF THE *ABBOTT* PRESCRIPTIONS

Early literacy was not a realistic objective as long as NJSC mandates hindered the implementation of effective practices. In April 2003, the New Jersey attorney general petitioned the NJSC to replace the many mandated remedies in *Abbott V* with a district-by-district approach that emphasized pedagogy and early literacy. The administration's filing leaned heavily on the certification of Fred Carrigg, who described the policies and practices of the Union City schools as a counter to the court's prescriptive remedies. The court dodged the request by mandating mediation between NJDOE and the Education Law Center (ELC). A month of intensive mediation produced a compromise that was accepted by the court as *Abbott X*. Basically, the parties reconfirmed the mandate for preschool, early literacy, and smaller classes, and modified the WSR mandate to permit up to half of the three hundred elementary schools to waive a WSR model. All other mandates became subject to a test of both need and effectiveness.

For the half of elementary schools that did not meet the specific conditions for dropping a WSR contract, NJDOE offered its Intensive Early Literacy (IEL) model as an acceptable alternative. Quietly, the Education Law Center accepted IEL as a surrogate Whole School Reform model. Despite plaintiffs' vigorous defense of WSR during mediation, no petitions were filed to force maintenance or adoption of WSR. By 2005, fewer than 20 percent of schools maintained formal WSR contracts.

Abbott X also ordered NJDOE to intervene in forty-two "low-performing schools" (LPS) where 50 percent or more of the unclassified fourth graders were not proficient on the 2002 state test for language arts. This appallingly low threshold was set intentionally to reflect NJDOE's limited organizational and intellectual resources. Each school was to be evaluated by a dedicated Performance Assessment Team that was to review the school's performance and order a plan and timetable for setting it on the right path. Handed down on June 24, 2003, *Abbott X* contemplated that these worst-performing schools would be cleaned up in the upcoming 2003–04 school year.

USING *ABBOTT X* TO RESTORE TO THE DISTRICT CENTRAL OFFICE RESPONSIBILITY FOR ACADEMIC RESULTS

Changes in classroom instruction cannot be mandated—if they could, the achievement gap long since would have been closed. Nor can the kind of paperwork exercise depicted in Box 8.2 (see page 70) produce the collegial and professional culture that characterizes effective schools and districts. Effectively, the *Abbott X* mandate granted NJDOE little more than "convening authority" to assemble the dozen affected districts and to gain the attention of the superintendent. It was up to district and school leaders to recognize the difficulty of the work facing classroom teachers and to support them in changing their teaching. In recognition of this essential fact, NJDOE used the authority granted it by *Abbott X* to offer an atypical deal to each of the twelve affected districts:

Box 8.2
The "Trenton-Knows-Best" Game

Abbott was entirely consistent with the top-down, we-know-best culture of education departments. With the NJSC decision promulgated June 24, 2003, in *Abbott X*, here is a *hypothetical* reaction if the department had followed its typical approach:

◆   First, districts would receive a memorandum announcing that the court had reached its decision, which would be attached to the memo, and that the twelve affected districts would have to attend the department's orientation on July 5 at 10:00 A.M. (BYO coffee).

◆   At the orientation, the assistant commissioner and the chief deputy attorney general would give a power point presentation to inform districts of procedures and deadlines. The first deadline would be July 31 (twenty-six days hence) by which time districts would have to return by fax the forms indicating that they had appointed Performance Assessment Teams (PATs) for each low-performing school (LPS). They would have to attach resumes and a statement signed by the superintendent certifying the process employed to ensure parent, teacher, and community representation.

◆   If approved by NJDOE, the PATs would conduct a review of all relevant data on student performance and compliance with the Abbott mandates, take a "walk-through" of the school once in session in September, and prepare a draft report for submission to NJDOE by October 1, 2003, detailing the nature of the educational problems, the program and remedies identified to correct those problems, the identification of the individual responsible for implementation, and a timetable to begin not later than October 31, 2003. The draft Performance Improvement Plan (PIP), in a form prescribed by NJDOE, would have to be be approved by the School Management Team (SMT), certified as acceptable by the superintendent, and approved by the district board of education. Notice of the SMT's meeting for consideration of the PIP would have to be circulated to all parents, teachers, and interested community members at least five days prior to the meeting. A copy of the notice would need to be attached to the PIP.

- If approved by NJDOE, the PAT would have to reconvene to conduct an Interim Progress Report (IPR), in a form prescribed by NJDOE, to be submitted to the SMT and the district office no later than February 15, 2004, specifying the interim goals that have been achieved and those that have not, and the explanations for non-compliance. A revised PIP would have to be attached to the IPR incorporating new schedules for PIP implementation.

- No later than July 1, 2004, the PAT and superintendent would have to submit the Annual Performance Improvement Plan Report (APIPR) to document the progress made by students in each LPS and to revise the PIP for the second year of implementation. The APIPR would have to include evidence from the NJASK3 and NJASK4 Language Arts examination for 2003–04 to demonstrate improvement by all subgroups (male, female, white, Asian, African American, Latino, special education, English-language learners, and students eligible for free or reduced lunches).

- The objective was to change classroom practice to improve early literacy, as measured by state tests. Implicit was an agreement that whatever was being done now in the low-performing schools (and most other schools for that matter) was not working.

- To start, the district was to provide achievement data by NCLB subgroups for at least three years. These data were to be jointly analyzed to reach a preliminary agreement specifying the major obstacles to literacy attainment at both the school and district level. No agreement, no next step.

- After conducting "walk-throughs" of each low-performing school, the district and NJDOE were to agree in writing to a prescription for improving classroom instruction school-by-school,

---

Box 8.3
SCHOOLS, BY THEMSELVES, HAVE NO CHANCE

Principals and teachers can do only so much by themselves. How can each school sort through the hundreds of Core Curriculum Content Standards, and why would any district want to end up with the resulting chaos? How can one school compare how well its fourth-grade African-American males perform with those in other schools in the district, and how can they determine what explains the variations? Only the district and state have these data. How does each school find effective Spanish-language materials that are aligned with the curricular standards? In the absence of frequent district assessments, how can schools track their achievement? Given the stagnant results in reading and writing, should the reading series be replaced with yet another textbook or with a combination of materials better targeted to the state's curricular standards? If so, where would schools find the time to analyze all the materials available? How would each school sort through all the instructional software programs, with their extravagant claims of efficacy? It is plainly unfair and delusional to expect already-busy teachers and principals to accomplish this kind of work.

---

including the role of the district in providing data, instructional materials, and teacher support.

◆   NJDOE provided whatever professional development was required, for example, help for teachers so that they can "differentiate" instruction in small groups or introduce better Spanish language materials in bilingual classes.

◆   As Intensive Early Literacy was implemented, NJDOE and the district would assess interim results to adjust instruction and teacher training.

THE BIG CHANGE—PARTNERSHIP

The instinct of bureaucrats, politicians, editorial writers, and many educators is to expect that a packaged and easily implemented answer can be identified and forced on unwilling or sluggish schools. "If it works in Union City, then mandate it for Camden" is the thinking. Futile thinking. The evidence is overwhelming that changes needed to introduce good pedagogy in struggling schools cannot be brought about by fiat. Both NCLB and Abbott make strong cases that top-down mandates intended to improve classroom results do not work.

A state education department that wants to influence classroom practice must instead adopt a collegial approach in the hope that the district headquarters staff accepts responsibility to help teachers change how they teach. Right now, most do not.

DISTRICT RESPONSIBILITY AND THE "80 PERCENT SOLUTION"

Abbott X gave NJDOE court-mandated entry to just twelve of the thirty-Abbott districts. That was the idea. In carrying out this mandate, NJDOE wanted to start with the districts with the most struggling students and schools. The twelve districts enrolled just 12.6 percent of the 100,000 or so fourth graders who had taken the 2003 literacy test, but accounted for 28.1 percent of those who failed. The other eighteen Abbott districts accounted for 6.3 percent of tested fourth graders and 11 percent of the "partially" proficient.[4] The idea of producing fourteen separate plans for fourteen different low-performing schools in Newark or six separate plans for six Camden schools made no sense. The Abbott division started with the superintendent to ensure district leadership and support, and to reverse the years of district office exile brought on by *Abbott V*.

For the typical school facing such typical problems, it is apparent that the district must bear the responsibility for providing a coherent instructional road map.[5] All the questions in Box 8.3 are best answered by the district staff, working with teachers, principals, and content specialists. Visits by the Abbott Division to under-performing city schools led to the conclusion that about 80 percent of the changes required to improve academic achievement rely on work that must be initiated by the district.

NJDOE outlined a quite specific set of responsibilities and tasks that had to be accepted and performed by the district central office for Intensive Early Literacy to work. The basic ingredients of IEL were intended to be followed in all Abbott districts, not just the twelve covered by *Abbott X*. These elements—borrowed unapologetically from Union City—were incorporated in the annual regulations of the Abbott Division, as well as in its less formal guidance documents, workshops, and symposia:

◆   It is the district that must adopt a comprehensive and uniform approach to teaching literacy, not a jumble of several WSR models or different basal readers. This involves much more than deciding on one of the commercial reading series, for it must incorporate the expectations from the core curriculum standards for language arts in each grade. This "mapping" of generalized curricular objectives with the instructional materials that best teach them should be a process that is continuous and involves teachers. In Abbott districts, the literacy curriculum must also reflect the expectations and curriculum from the preschool program, which now serves about 70 percent of all entering kindergarteners.

◆   It is the district that must ensure that every school and classroom is offering a minimum ninety minutes of uninterrupted literacy instruction in grades K–3 at least, and more for English learners. Again, it is simple to mandate this minimum, but it is a very different thing to prepare teachers for making the change. Integral to this requirement is the use of small-group instruction for reading, writing, and computers, through which students with similar pedagogical problems are grouped for twenty or so minutes of targeted instruction daily. Educators call this "differentiated, " instruction. When computer centers are used for this instruction, the district must identify the software that is aligned with the literacy curriculum; many districts leave the selection to "technology coordinators" or individual teachers.

◆   It is the district that must provide the budget and coherence for ensuring that there are libraries in every primary classroom with at least 300 titles. The library for one second grade class may be very different from others, depending on the class makeup and achievement levels. The district must assure that native-language texts are available for English learners and that they are age appropriate (a thirteen-year-old Mexican immigrant illiterate in Spanish will not be enamored of a *Three Bears* diet). Teachers should be invited to select some of the titles that they have found most engaging and effective.

◆ It is the district that must do what it takes to guarantee that all students who fall behind will receive whatever extra attention they need to become literate third graders. Ninety minutes daily is often not enough time for teachers to diagnose the problem and work more closely with the student. This is, partly, a budget issue, but it is much more a concern that the extra time required be meshed with the classroom experience. Ideally, a before- or after-school session will be taught by the student's regular teacher. The special help may involve nonpedagogical assistance, such as dealing with an asthma or nutritional problem.

◆ It is the district that must guarantee that the class size mandates of the *Abbott* V and X decisions are realized and fully funded, that is, fifteen for preschool, twenty-one for K-3.

◆ It is the district that must develop common, frequent, and interim assessments of student progress (in addition to annual state tests and measures by teachers). Such screening is essential for organizing small group instruction. The results of these assessments must be scrutinized to determine patterns among schools, within schools, within grade levels, and within content areas. If, for example, 86 percent of third graders district-wide miss question number fourteen on the eight-week test, it is the district that should organize the adjustments required to teach the relevant content. Results for each student must be shared with teachers and principals and an interim instructional plan drawn up to deal with individual weaknesses.

◆ It is the district that must maintain a student-level database to track all assessments and produce individual student and comparative performance data presented in an accessible form for teacher and principal use.

◆ It is the district that must assume the responsibility to reduce the segregation of special education students. Specifically, this means helping "general" teachers to deal with special education students, sometimes without a special education teacher to assist.

◆   Where the number of Latino students is growing, it is the district
    that must implement a common standard for assessing and placing
    Spanish-speakers.

◆   The quality of preschool instruction must be improved and the expe-
    riences of four-year-olds closely tied to the curriculum and practices
    in kindergarten and first grade. This is a particularly difficult objec-
    tive to achieve in districts that contract with many community and
    for-profit providers (for example, about 80 percent of Newark's
    5,500 preschoolers go to about sixty sites, operated by fifty different
    organizations).

Other issues may arise, but the NJDOE IEL framework anticipates
problems common to almost all city districts that can be solved only with
district leadership and management. Hence, the 80 percent estimate.

EARLY LITERACY AND RELUCTANT SUPERINTENDENTS

Abbott superintendents had good reason to be skeptical of proffers of assistance and cooperation from NJDOE. Almost all of the department-dis-
trict relationships had been adversarial, with one-way orders, deadlines,
and paperwork. It is not surprising that it took two or three years for
some superintendents to accept the deal; some never did (with negative
consequences for the students in their districts). They saw Abbott X as
another bureaucratic exercise—"here we go again." They were polite
and friendly, but that is not the same as agreeing to change instruction.
Just producing the longitudinal data in the form requested (and already
required by NCLB) took almost a year in Trenton and Camden. Meetings
to review findings and implications often were repeatedly postponed.
Even if NJDOE and a district agreed on the diagnosis of the district's literacy problem, some districts balked at actually undertaking any changes
in classroom practices. In some districts, principals were not informed of
school reviews or professional development sessions that had been sched-
uled through the central office. Amicably reached agreements disappeared
in fogs of forgetfulness, failed communication, and "local developments."
Resistant superintendents must have wondered: "Why provoke all the
contention that comes with changing what principals and teachers do if it
can be avoided without serious negative consequences?"[6]

Moreover, these same superintendents must have wondered why, after years of only issuing orders and conducting compliance reviews, should NJDOE be expected to add any value to the work of struggling schools? Even if built on the superior results of Union City, which were widely recognized by other Abbott districts, how could the expertise of a single educator, Fred Carrigg, be transferred to school districts that were much larger and heavily African-American? And, why would the NJDOE not use the information that it gained from this collaborative effort to justify slowing the rate of increase in, or even reducing, Abbott district budgets? Initially, Newark, Paterson, Trenton, and Camden declined to cooperate (twenty-seven of the forty-two low-performing schools were in these districts); Jersey City, Elizabeth, and six smaller districts quickly accepted.

The Abbott Division sought a district-led effort to change classroom practices and alter the prevailing culture in these schools. The most important change was one that would produce persistent, built-in concern over students who were not at standard, via the continuous collection and analysis of the evidence of their work and constant adjustments to teaching based on the results.

The city of Orange is an example of what this focused attention to classroom instruction can produce. It has ten schools and about five thousand students. With a small but growing Haitian and Latino population, it is 83 percent African-American, and over 71 percent of its students are eligible for free or reduced lunch (it is the eighth-poorest of the thirty-one Abbott districts). By 2002, there was no clear pattern to student achievement—Orange's highest-performing school served its poorest neighborhood. Orange ranked twenty-fifth on the list of thirty Abbott districts when the fourth grade literacy test was first administered in 1999—with a terrifyingly low 22 percent proficiency rate; by 2007, Orange students had climbed to the rank of fifth. With more than 75 percent proficiency in 2007, its fourth graders were close to the state average of 80 percent. This dramatic and sustained gap-closing is particularly important because it eliminated the "only-Latino-districts-can-achieve" excuse of majority black districts.

With a new superintendent in 2002, Orange worked closely with NJDOE to diagnose its problems school-by-school, adopted a comprehensive reading program that reflected the department's early literacy framework: classroom libraries, extended teaching time for literacy, extra attention for struggling readers, native language instruction for English learners, and small-group instruction for students with similar problems. Visits to primary grade classes today confirm that teachers know how to use nationally normed assessments to identify individual student weaknesses. A school-wide committee that includes teachers, coaches, and the school "facilitator" meets twice weekly to discuss the problems of individual students and to agree on concrete steps to be taken. Students talk freely of the books they select from the classroom library for independent reading and how they use the Internet to gather information for their research papers. What is most obvious is the shared focus on academics, the continuous use of evidence from student work, and the attention given to struggling students.

Two other smaller districts—Pleasantville and Asbury Park—responded quickly to the early literacy effort, and both districts showed significant improvement, primarily because teachers were given support in the teaching of writing. On the fourth grade 2004 literacy tests, Pleasantville improved by 19.7 percent and Asbury Park by 14.6 percent (Pleasantville has sustained these gains and improved on them; Asbury has fallen back, after a putsch of its middle management that drove their efforts off course). Both districts are majority African-American, with rapidly growing Latino enrollments.

Elizabeth, the state's fourth-largest district and the sixth-poorest Abbott district, with three-quarters of its students eligible for free or reduced lunch, proved that dramatic improvements were not limited to smaller districts. Long before *Abbott X*, Elizabeth's long-time superintendent, unlike many of his peers, moved to give preschool a special emphasis, including district operation of most classrooms. (In other large districts, leadership contracted with community day care providers to supply most classrooms, partly because of limited facilities.) Elizabeth also connected the preschool experience of four-year-olds to the kindergarten and first grade curriculum. In just four years, its third grade performance improved from 59 percent to 75 percent proficiency, far out-performing other large districts and many more affluent Abbott and other districts (the state average was 83 percent).

As word of the early successes in Orange, Pleasantville, and Asbury Park spread, Abbott districts that were not required to participate in IEL by Abbott X sought the help of Fred Carrigg and his colleagues. Plainfield needed help with its growing Latino population, Passaic with introducing small-group instruction, and Perth Amboy with middle grades literacy. Even as Camden, Trenton, and Paterson continued to resist implementation of basic IEL practices, Keansburg, Salem City, Vineland, New Brunswick, Pemberton, and Harrison sought and received district-specific assistance from the Abbott Division. Other smaller districts with noticeable problems politely rejected offers of help (Gloucester City, Burlington City, Neptune, Millville, and Phillipsburg). On the other hand, Newark adopted a much more cooperative spirit after a year of polite resistance.

MEASURING THE EFFECTS OF INTENSIVE EARLY LITERACY EFFORTS

"So what?" a Missourian might ask. "What did all this money, targeting of young students, and putative cooperation produce?" Fair enough. The short answer is: it depends on how energetically and coherently the district leadership focused on early literacy.

Figure 8.1 (see page 80) is a scatter graph that plots two bits of information for each Abbott district—the percentage of students eligible for free or reduced lunch, and the performance of their fourth graders on the 2007 language arts test. For four decades, we were accustomed to seeing a near-perfect relationship: the higher the poverty rate, the lower the achievement. What stands out immediately are the four districts in the upper right quadrant—high-achieving high-poverty districts (and West New York is nearly in that quadrant). It is not a one-year coincidence that Elizabeth, Orange, Perth Amboy, and Union City are in the upper right quadrant—both their poverty and achievement rates have remained relatively high over at least the past four years.

The solution to lagging achievement in each case is to start early in closing the kindergarten gap and to practice good pedagogy. This is simple to describe, but very difficult to carry out.

FIGURE 8.1 ABBOTT DISTRICT SCHOOLS, BY PERCENTAGE OF STUDENTS ELIGIBLE
FOR FREE OR REDUCED PRICE LUNCH AND PERFORMANCE ON THE FOURTH GRADE
LANGUAGE ARTS LITERACY TEST, 2007

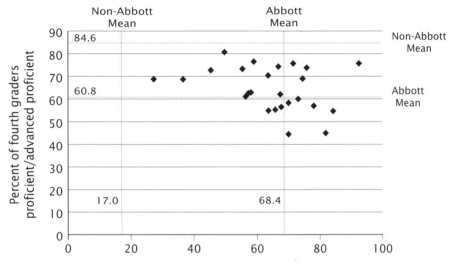

Percent of students eligible for free/reduced price meals

Notes: Data excludes districts in which fewer than 175 students tested: Burlington City,
Gloucester City, Harrison, Hoboken, Keansburg, and Salem City.
Source: Authors calculations from New Jersey Department of Education reports on statewide
assessments and enrollment for 2007.

Since New Jersey's Intensive Early Literacy program is really a
set of practices and habits built around classroom support and tailored help for struggling students, there is no ready formula or simple
answer to the question of which districts are most fully implementing it. This recognition will disappoint those seeking a successor to
Standards-based Instruction, Whole School Reform, School Choice, or
other nostrums that have failed to satisfy the search for the definitive
solution to the achievement gap. Just as good pedagogy ordains that
a teacher reflect on the evidence produced by each student to address
individual weaknesses, so must the best available evidence be weighed
to sort Abbott districts into those that are serious about IEL, those that
are serious but incomplete or late in their adoption of IEL practices,
and those that are indifferent. There are four sources of information
that the Abbott Division used to categorize districts to compare their
student performance.

The first source is the information adduced from four years of face-to-face meetings about academic performance held at least annually with each Abbott district. Each of the 120-plus meetings began with the question of how well primary grade students were reading and writing. Conducted as a Socratic dialogue, the purpose of these meetings was to gauge the most likely explanation for student performance and the quality of instructional leadership at the district level, and to determine if NJDOE could provide assistance. Here is a sample of the questions typically posed in the face-to-face:

- Does the district use a student database to analyze student performance information on state and interim district tests, and are those analyses shared in a timely way with schools and teachers to adjust instruction?

- How is the district curriculum revised to reflect changes in state academic standards and to specify expectations for early literacy in the primary grades?

- How are Spanish-speaking immigrants screened for literacy in their first language, and what range of bilingual instruction is available to them?

- What extra assistance is given struggling students beyond that possible during the literacy block (required to be at least ninety minutes of uninterrupted instruction)? Is it given before or after school, during lunch hour, or at the expense of other subjects?

- If the district is introducing small-group instruction in the primary grades, how much professional development and in-class support is given teachers? What has the district learned that requires adjustments district-wide, in particular schools, at particular grade levels, in individual classrooms, and so on?

The idea of the face-to-face was to engage in a two-hour, data-driven conversation about pedagogy and student performance, and nothing else. The objective was to reach agreement on the two or three instructional problems that should receive the district's most fervent attention, captured in a summary letter.

Second, in the twelve districts covered by *Abbott X*, which enrolled 65.2 percent of all Abbott students, there was a more intensive and detailed review of early literacy practices. As described earlier, each district participated in the analyses of performance data and in reaching preliminary diagnoses for each school. It also helped shape the content, frequency, and magnitude of the professional development required to improve pedagogy. This process revealed a great deal about the competence and focus of district leadership. For example:

◆   A district might purchase a minimum of three hundred titles for each classroom, but the walk-through could find that the books have not been distributed, or that they showed little evidence of use.

◆   Professional development sessions, which should be attended by school administrators, produce an inconsistent pattern of attendance, with few principals participating in all sessions.

◆   The district central office staff may analyze interim assessment data rigorously, but fail to share it in a timely or usable form with school administrators and teachers.

A particularly helpful indicator of district leadership was the pace at which the district responded to the opportunity to strengthen early literacy. A delay in providing easily available data on student subgroup performance as required for NCLB reflects low priority assigned by district leadership. The pattern of inconsistent participation by the principals of low-performing schools in the professional development sessions designed to deal with their school's documented problems is also revealing. A reluctance by the district office to work cooperatively with school leaders and teachers, opting for a command-and-obey culture, was a tip-off to major obstacles to improving pedagogy.

Third, and following on the second source, is the school "walk-throughs" and training programs conducted by NJDOE's literacy staff, particularly in the schools and districts specified in *Abbott X*. Spending an hour or so during the literacy block looking at whether the program is being implemented can reveal a lot about the extent to which a new instructional culture is being created in failing schools. Here is what is obvious: the districts in which fourth graders demonstrated the greatest improvement in reading and writing in the five years beginning in 2003 were those that were most diligent in implementing NJDOE's early literacy framework.[7] What is also quite clear is that a spirit of cooperation and good intentions, by themselves, were not enough to produce significant improvement. Sadly, for some students, a convincing case can be made that reading and writing skills improved least, or actually declined, among fourth graders in the least cooperative districts, particularly Camden, Trenton, and Paterson.

NJDOE professional development was tailored to the needs of each district, based on the kind of review specified for *Abbott X* districts. As practices improved, the character and intensity of training would be adjusted. If teachers in one district could not administer diagnostic instruments to place their students for small-group instruction, then they would be trained in their use before turning to how to target instruction in small-group settings to each student's weaknesses. The next year's training might focus on how to increase and improve the quality of the students' writing. In another district, where early literacy was more advanced, NJDOE's training might be focused on the application of early literacy practices to the needs of special education students, or how to incorporate classroom library books into research/writing projects that integrate social studies content with literacy.

Fourth, the special effort launched with the full cooperation of the NJDOE Office of Special Education (described in detail in Chapter 9) provides another source of information about the relative seriousness or passivity of Abbott districts. This initiative offered districts the opportunity to integrate disabled students into IEL more fully. For many districts, this marked a sharp departure from past practice, which had segregated the disabled from their unclassified classmates. Basically, many urban districts did not accept that disabled students had the cognitive capacity to master any part of the required curriculum, an assertion justified by their appallingly low performance on state assessments.

This is a lot of information to sort and reflect on, and not all of it is subject to counting and measurement. For example, do all second graders spend at least ninety uninterrupted minutes on literacy or are there three hundred titles in their classroom library? Do districts use interim assessments that are used to adjust instruction to meet the individual academic needs of students? But it is important to note that simply adopting the forms of IEL is not a guarantee, or even a reasonable assurance, that classroom practice will improve.

The primary measure of the impact of IEL implementation are the results from the state fourth grade language arts test, stated as a percentage of students who are proficient or advanced proficient. This indicator carries all the usual problems of standardized tests: year-to-year changes in the difficulty of the tests, the number of fourth graders tested can be quite small or vary noticeably, the demographic/economic changes in student characteristics, and so on. The blurring of "proficient" with "advanced proficient," or not using the mean scale score, robs the analysis of richness (for example, districts that aim at maximizing performance around the proficient cut score of 200 versus those that seek to move more students to "advanced proficient" status). All that said, there is no other uniform, reasonably consistent, and universal measure available.

So, how did the individual districts do in implementing IEL? Perhaps the most crucial examination can be made in the twelve districts that were directed by the Supreme Court in *Abbott X* to work with NJDOE to improve instruction in their forty-two low-performing schools. These twelve districts can be been grouped by their relative energy in adopting early literacy as a priority, in cooperating with NJDOE, and in using the professional development opportunities offered by the department.

Four districts—Orange, Pleasantville, Elizabeth, and Jersey City—are judged to be "high" implementers of IEL. This means that each of these districts undertook an intelligent, focused, and data-driven effort at the district level to support changes in classroom practice for all students. The distinction between "high" and "medium" is the intensity of focus by the district leadership on the most serious pedagogical issues. For example, in Orange, emphasis was given to the development and implementation of a coherent and comprehensive reading/writing curricula for all schools. In Elizabeth, particular attention was given to English learners. Jersey City focused on how to intensify small-group instruction and to give more time to the needs of struggling readers. Pleasantville concentrated on writing.

Five districts—Asbury Park, Bridgeton, East Orange, Irvington, and Newark—are judged to be "medium" implementers. They are districts that might have delayed their buy-in of IEL practices (Newark and Bridgeton, for example), or might not have focused on particular subgroups of students (Irvington did not attack problems of English learners), or might have had implementation fall off after an initial burst (Asbury Park, for example). Three districts—Camden, Paterson, and Trenton—are characterized as "low" implementers. In these districts, literacy was treated as another exercise with the NJDOE, not the opportunity to make all primary students strong readers. No sense of urgency was set by the front office, and that message was received clearly at the school level.

Figure 8.2 (see page 86) suggests that the 2004 and 2005 tests might have been less difficult than the 2003 edition (a new vendor introduced a new test in 2004 that is portrayed as psychometrically consistent with 2003). What is most apparent is that high implementing districts held the gains achieved in 2004; the other eight *Abbott X* districts did not. This gap would have been wider had Jersey City's performance in 2006 and 2007 not fallen noticeably from 2005. It is also noticeable that the districts with the biggest gaps—Camden, Paterson, Trenton—were the least active in changing classroom practice. They started and stayed low. Why? Concentrated poverty is one possible explanation. When looking at the percentage of students eligible for free lunch, Camden (65.4 percent) and Paterson (67.9 percent) are very poor; Trenton (54.6 percent), however, is modestly poor by contrast. However, Elizabeth (64.0 percent) and Newark (63.5 percent) are close behind Camden—so the difference is not definitive.[8]

Another significant finding from the data is that the eighteen districts not covered by *Abbott X* made the most progress over the five years. There are several explanations that make sense. First, four of the seven largest districts of the eighteen—Union City, West New York, Vineland, Perth Amboy—are strong practitioners of IEL. When combined with Pemberton, another "high" implementer, the students in those five districts amounted to 41.5 percent of the proficient students overall. They enjoyed consistent and sustained gains at high levels (75 percent of their fourth graders were proficient or advance proficient in 2007 versus 60.4 percent for the other

FIGURE 8.2 PERCENTAGE OF ABBOTT X DISTRICT FOURTH GRADERS PROFICIENT/
ADVANCED PROFICIENT ON STATE LITERACY TESTS, BY DEGREE OF IMPLEMENTATION
OF EARLY LITERACY, COMPARED TO NON-ABBOTT AND OTHER ABBOTT STUDENTS,
2003-2007

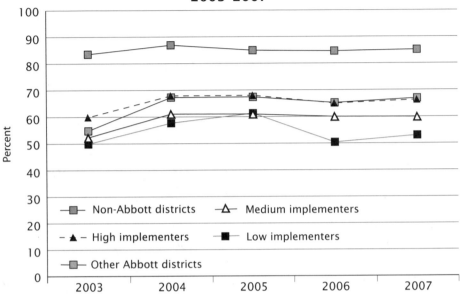

Note: In two Camden elementary schools, NJDOE reported evidence of "adult interference," which may explain the dramatic increases in proficiency rates in those schools in
the "low" implementers category for 2005.

Source: Author calculations from annual reports by the New Jersey Department of
Education, "Grade 4 Assessment of Skills and Knowledge," for 2003–2007.

twenty-six Abbotts). Second, to the extent that there are "more affluent"
Abbott districts, they are found in this "other" group. Six of the eighteen,
all relatively small, have a free lunch incidence below 40 percent; four
of these are below 30 percent. Third, Garfield, which employs a highly
decentralized, teacher-run approach, and Long Branch, which remains
faithful to a modified Success for All curriculum, are consistently high-
performing districts.[9]

The pattern in too many districts was depressingly similar: special
education students and English learners were left out of the discussion,
with predictably lousy results. It is to these problems we now turn.

9

SPECIAL EDUCATION STUDENTS
AND ENGLISH-LANGUAGE LEARNERS

The 1966 Coleman Report famously documented that the social-economic-educational background of one's parents most strongly explained variations in academic performance. But the second most important explanation was the socioeconomic status of the students with whom one goes to school. In other words, children learn not only from their parents and teachers, but also from their fellow students. Ever since Coleman, educational policies have leaned to inclusion rather than separation: the notion of including children with problems in classes of children without such problems has been considered good policy, and pulling them out of "general" classrooms and segregating them with other kids with the same problems has been considered bad policy.

About one-third of Abbott district students are either disabled, still learning English, or both. Yet, English-language learners (ELL) were ignored altogether in the Abbott arguments and decisions; special education students were at least recognized as having needs that might not be satisfied by the Abbott remedies. The slight attention paid by the New Jersey Supreme Court (NJSC) mirrors the practice in too many city districts, where the labels of "disabled" or "ELL" are permits to segregate, isolate, and to shrug: "Hey, what can you expect?"

Legal and Programmatic Contexts of Special Education

The framework for special education is set in federal law, specifically the Individuals with Disabilities Education Act (IDEA), enacted in 1975, and subsequent revisions and reauthorizations, regulations, and federal court decisions. It is the one area of public education where policy and practice are both controlled largely by the federal government. Special education has evolved into a highly regimented, legalistic system that prizes process, parental participation, and paperwork.

Federal policy blends conflicting notions of pedagogy and expectations. Special education law employs a medical model, in which teams of specialists provide individualized diagnoses of highly specific disabilities, and in turn produce individualized education plans (IEPs) to guide instruction. This model assumes a level of scientific rigor that simply does not exist. In fact, the largest category of special education students is the imprecise, even mushy "specific learning disability." While the IEP presumes that every student's under-performance can be explained by a diagnosable cause that, in turn, can be addressed by specialized instruction, federal policy now recognizes the value of disabled students learning from their general education classmates. States now are expected to "mainstream" almost all disabled students into general education classrooms, with the exception of those with disabilities such as severe autism or Down syndrome who require separate classes or institutions.

Separateness and Segregation

The pattern in many Abbott districts is all too clear: many students who lag in reading are referred to the child study teams for classification and eventual segregation. Interestingly, districts with strong early literacy results tend to have dramatically lower classification rates.[1] In too many districts, however, there is a separate curriculum for special education that is not aligned to the state academic standards and tests. Special education teachers are frequently left out of professional development sessions on content and practice.

The classification of special education students follows certain racial fault lines: black students are (moderately) more likely to be classified than white, Asian, or Latino students (in 2006, blacks were 17.4 percent of all New Jersey students, but 22 percent of those classified). The dramatic difference is what happens to them after classification. Over half (51.5 percent) of disabled white students spend 80 percent or more of their time in general education classrooms; only 27.8 percent of black students are similarly integrated, and they are much more likely to be shipped out of district for instruction (10.5 percent for blacks versus 6.3 percent for whites).[2]

In a discipline premised on a scientific approach, one might expect reasonable consistency in how disabled students are classified and educated. Instead, there are wild variations district to district, even when the student profile is similar. New Jersey is no different from other states in this respect. The National Academy of Sciences concluded: "There is a great deal of variability from place to place in the criteria used to define disability, the financial incentives and disincentives for classification, and in the local implementing conditions for deciding who qualifies as having a disability."[3] After three or so years of segregation, most disabled students are hopelessly behind their peers, and doomed to a substandard education. Smaller classes for disabled students are intended to improve pedagogy. In fact, as teachers naturally focus on the lowest-performing students out of six or eight in a "resource room," those of greater cognition are left with less and less stimulation and more boredom.

By definition, we would expect disabled students to struggle to attain proficiency on state tests. They do. While they comprise one out of six of all Abbott students, they are one-third of those not proficient. Only 25 percent of Abbott fourth grade disabled students were proficient on the 2006 language arts literacy test, compared to 55 percent in non-Abbott districts. The classification rate was 15.1 percent for both. By eighth grade, however, the Abbott classification rate climbs to one in five (19.6 percent), while proficiency declines to about one in ten (11.7 percent). By contrast, 39.3 percent of non-Abbott eighth grade disabled students are proficient, with the classification rate holding at 15.1 percent.

Working closely with the New Jersey Department of Education (NJDOE) special education office, the leadership of which was anxious to attack this syndrome, districts were offered redirected federal funds to hire special education literacy specialists. The aim was to introduce the practices of Intensive Early Literacy (IEL) to disabled students. All but two districts accepted in the first year.[4] The offices of special education and urban literacy organized an intensive summer training session with fall and spring follow-ups. Launched in the 2005–06 school year, the response by districts has been effusive, but that has not translated into significant improvements in test results (the 2007 third grade results improved by six percentage points, to 32 percent proficiency, close to the results two years earlier). However, the experience in individual districts suggests that the state's approach can work. Five very different districts—Vineland, Perth Amboy, Orange, Union City, and Long Branch—have achieved significantly improved results with their special education students on the 2007 tests.[5]

Most educators do not expect much from special education students. They are rarely disappointed. Other educators see greater cognitive potential in special education students. They are usually rewarded.

THE EVEN MORE CONFUSING WORLD OF BILINGUAL EDUCATION

In their recent book, *The American Dream and the Public Schools*, Jennifer Hochschild and Nathan Scovronick make an important observation: "While most of those who promote civil rights for special education students call for more or complete inclusion, most who seek civil rights for English learners endorse longer or more complete separation from mainstream classes."[6] English-language learners are set off by other noticeable differences:

◆   many, but not most, are immigrants, and many of them are illegal aliens;

◆   they have been concentrated in a few states and a few cities within those states until recently (in the early 1990s, California, Texas, New York, Florida, Illinois, and New Jersey accounted for half of all English learners[7]);

◆   they come from much poorer households than average students; and

◆   the best way to educate them is the subject of intense political debate and, even, referenda.

What special education and English acquisition share is that academic research and evaluation does not resolve what works best. Again, from Hochschild and Scovronick: "The reasons are familiar: different programs fall under the vague rubric of bilingual education; the quality of programs and teachers is mixed; characteristics of English-language learners are extremely variable; testing has often been unfair, inappropriate, or limited; and program evaluations have been badly done or too politicized to permit reliable conclusions."[8]

New Jersey's experience with English-language learners reflects the nation's increasingly Latino accent. In the nine years from 1998 to 2006, the number of Latino students grew by 43.8 percent, from 14.3 percent of all students to 18.9 percent. Latinos now are the majority minority both statewide and in the Abbott districts (40.9 percent Latino versus 39.8 percent African-American).

It may not be surprising, but the districts where Latino students performed best tended to be those where Latinos had significant political influence. In Union City and West New York, Latinization began with Cuban Americans who, initially, were not only middle-class refugees from Fidel Castro, but also eligible for American citizenship. In Perth Amboy and Newark, the largest Latino population was Puerto Ricans, and thus were automatic citizens. In recent years, more immigrants are coming from the Dominican Republic and Mexico, followed by Central America (primarily Hondurans, Salvadorans, and Guatemalans). Many of the newcomers are undocumented. The road to citizenship is slow, even for those who entered the United States legally, and unavailable to illegal immigrants. Moreover, Abbott districts are losing their Latino "market share": between 1998 and 2006, the percentage of New Jersey's total Latino students in other districts climbed from 40.7 percent to 56.3 percent. The consequence is diluted political influence town-by-town.

Paterson is a good example of the phenomenon of Latinization—a port of entry for Central American, Dominican, and Peruvian immigrants, reflected in its 55 percent Latino enrollment (plus 10 percent Palestinian and Syrian). Paterson's school board, however, is majority African-American, as is practically all of its district senior management. Only 30 percent of Paterson's fourth graders categorized as English-language learners were proficient on the 2007 language arts literacy test versus 42 percent of Abbott's English-language learners. Newark, Elizabeth, and Union City have visible Latino leadership at the school board and city level and have had the highest levels of English-language learner proficiency (55 percent, 48 percent, and 58 percent, respectively). The relationship of political power to improved instruction is not absolute, however: Passaic has a Latino mayor and a Latino majority school board, but produces only a 25 percent proficiency rate for English-language learners.

Two mid-size Abbott districts, Plainfield and New Brunswick, reflect the tide of Latino growth. In the eight years since 1998, the number of African-American students in Plainfield declined by 43 percent, while the number of Latinos doubled (they now make up 40 percent of total enrollment). Yet, on the homepage of the Plainfield district Web site, only the bilingual program offers Spanish language assistance. The Plainfield Board of Education includes one Latino and eight African Americans, and the administration is almost entirely black. During this surge in Latino growth, Plainfield's comparative performance on fourth grade language declined from eighteenth to twenty-seventh among Abbott districts, trailing the larger and poorer cities of Paterson, Elizabeth, Newark, and Jersey City. Plainfield's black students do noticeably better than black students in Abbott districts; its Latinos do noticeably worse. When the then-superintendent was asked in 2006 why this was so, her answer was quick and discouraging: the district leadership did not know what to do.

New Brunswick has gone through a similar change, with black students declining by one-third since 1998, while Latinos increased by 85 percent. In the 2006–07 school year, Latinos were 75 percent of all students, with most of the growth explained by Mexican immigrants. Its mayor-appointed, seven-member board of education includes two Latinos, but its Web site includes no guidance for Spanish-only readers. Until recently, each principal was free to determine what instructional approach to use to deal with growing numbers of Latino immigrants. One principal adopted a "Spanish-only" regime, another "English immersion." The result was chaos and consistently poor results.

New Jersey is one of nine states that mandate bilingual instruction in districts with more than twenty students of one foreign language. But the law was amended to give parents the right to withdraw their children from bilingual instruction and to permit the NJDOE to grant waivers, which it has done liberally. The districts in which Spanish-speakers do best, such as Union City and West New York, seek to educate genuinely bilingual students. Their highest-performing subgroup is students who have completed the districts' English-language learner programs.

Much of Union City's success can be attributed to Fred Carrigg, who began his management career as the city's supervisor of bilingual education. A Spanish major at Montclair State, he was an active participant in the New Jersey association of bilingual instructors and an adjunct professor at his alma mater. He is a strong proponent of the idea that non-English speaking students need to gain knowledge and vocabulary in their first language, especially when they are young, if they are to succeed in learning English and succeed academically. If they become literate in, say, Spanish, then the bridge to English mastery is much stronger because their general knowledge is greater and they can connect written and oral languages.

It is not surprising, then, that after being brought in by the NJDOE in 2002, Carrigg paid careful attention to the instructional practices of all Abbott districts when it came to how their Spanish-speaking students were diagnosed and instructed. His personal and professional interest coincided perfectly with the Latinization of so many city districts and the increased visibility English-language learners received as a result of the No Child Left Behind Act (NCLB). Elizabeth, Jersey City, and, later, New Brunswick, Plainfield, and Passaic were particularly anxious to adopt the Union City approach to teaching English.

10

LESSONS LEARNED IN ATTEMPTING TO CLOSE THE ACHIEVEMENT GAP

Education reform has failed to close the achievement gap between students in poor districts and their more affluent cohorts for a lot of reasons, but some are more important than others. Public education is too complex, too scattered across fifty nearly sovereign state systems, and too locked into mountains of well-intentioned and inconsistent laws, regulations, and policies to ever be reformed. After half a century of commission reports, crusades, and "wars on . . . ," and with trillions of dollars already spent, we should acknowledge that "systemic" structural changes are not working. There are two exceptions over that fifty-year period: the end of de jure segregation, and federal special education legislation.[1] Otherwise, the notion that Congress, federal bureaucrats, foundation-funded commissions, or flamboyant entrepreneurs can deeply influence classroom pedagogy should be dismissed.

Despite their well-intentioned efforts, reformers have often overlooked—or even created—serious obstacles to improving the academic performance of children in poor school districts. Poor policy choices have led to a situation in which even the best teachers and administrators struggle in educating the students in their charge.

Seven Big Things That Have Gone Wrong

1. The challenge of educating poor children in poor districts must be the starting point—it usually has not been.

Reformers almost always invoke improving student achievement as the rationale for their proposals. However, their plans usually push for changes that are unconnected to the pedagogical needs of teachers and students and make no effort to improve teacher-student interaction. Since most poor minority students are not sufficiently educated to graduate from high school, let alone succeed at the university level, we can conclude that their cumulative classroom experiences were insufficient. If we do not change these experiences for both students and teachers, then we are living Einstein's definition of insanity: doing the same thing over and over while expecting different results.

There are many reasons that reformers avoid changing classroom interaction. To revise a quote from the late Speaker of the House, Thomas "Tip" O'Neill, "all education is local, very local." Yet national policy debates take place at 30,000 feet and typically overlook the semi-sovereign status of state governments when it comes to setting the ground rules for education. The No Child Left Behind Act (NCLB) is the perfect example of a sensible policy objective—improved accountability—reduced to hash by the exercise of the educational equivalent of Enron accounting. In their attempt to comply with NCLB, most states adopted too many standards, many of which were too soft, too vague, too specific, too general, or lacking in rigor. Weak academic standards produced appallingly low testing standards that eviscerated any reasonable notion of accountability.

The simplistic, formulaic, mechanical answers preferred by the "big picture" reformers just will not do. What will do is professional reflection and assessment, a difficult process and one for which most teachers are unprepared. Faced with such an untidy task and the enormity of the changes required, it is no surprise that reformers fall back on insubstantial proposals, such as shifting a few students to different schools (vouchers, magnet, and charter schools), or changing procedures (school-based budgeting), or tackling relevant but long-term issues (leadership development, teacher preparation), or avoiding the issue altogether (Ebonics, distance learning).

A caution about teacher-bashing. Since the theme of this story is the need to change classroom instruction, some may be encouraged to blame teachers for the persistent achievement gap. Yes, there are bad, uninspired, under-prepared teachers. Yes, tenure laws and labor contracts make it difficult to rid schools of such teachers. Yes, we need better-prepared and better-mentored teachers. No, the problem cannot be solved by even the best-motivated, energetic, intelligent teachers operating alone. No teacher can sort through numerous and often imprecise state curricular standards or the state assessments and divine from them the concrete implications for the content, sequencing, or pacing of what is to be taught, and how. Even great teachers need assistance to confront pedagogical puzzles. While proposals to "improve the breed" of teachers are welcome[2] (as are those that attack other long-term, structural weaknesses in public education), city students are owed answers that can be provided by today's teachers and administrators.

2. Teachers have not spent enough time with students who struggle.

Teachers are under enormous pressure to teach more skills and content than kids can absorb in 180 six-hour days per school year. As they present new material to the whole class, they ask questions and encourage questions. When the right answers are given, often by the same five or six students, teachers assume the material has been adequately mastered, and move on. Particularly in the early years of education, it is essential that no child be left behind, not if all students are expected to be literate. When the Broad Foundation and the Bill and Melinda Gates Foundation set up a national effort—Strong American Schools—to elevate public education as an issue in the 2008 presidential campaign, they sensibly focused on three goals: strong standards, effective teachers, and more time and support for learning.[3] Not all kids learn at the same time and in the same way, which is why taking extra time to work on individual problems is fundamental to improved pedagogy.

3. Small-scale triumphs have been confused for generalized solutions.

Rather than take on the wholesale intellectual burdens of assessing individual student needs in each classroom, reformers run boutiques. The proponents of neat ideas assume that if they can demonstrate results on a small scale, then somehow the idea can be introduced universally to solve an underlying problem. Vouchers, charter schools, "metro busing," and magnet programs are examples of "10 percent solutions"—they do no more than improve the prospects for a small portion of students. Many

foundations seem to operate on the assumption that their comparatively puny grants to introduce, say, laptops at PS #12 somehow will
produce, after just three years, a self-financed expansion to all schools.
KIPP academies report dramatic results from recruiting students from
motivated families; extending the school day by two hours, the school
week by a half-day Saturday, and adding four weeks to the school year;
recruiting bright young teachers who agree to longer hours; and focusing relentlessly on academics.

Such efforts are not to be denigrated but rather to be commended
when they are effective and replicated whenever possible. However,
they should not be confused with strategies aimed at addressing the
instructional needs of all students in all schools and working with all
teachers.

4. National and state policies in the 1990s drifted toward the notion that the central headquarters of urban districts could not be trusted to act on behalf of students' interests.

As documented in the discussion of Whole School Reform (WSR)
in Chapter 7, its proponents dismissed district-level initiatives for a
school-by-school effort. Bureaucracy, corruption, incompetence, and
political interference in district offices were offered as the justification
for WSR. Business leaders and former governors organized a national
competition to entice corporations, academics, nonprofits, and others
to propose "models" of reform. There was no recognition that districts
existed, or could play even a supporting role in the education of students.

The district leadership must accept responsibility for academic
achievement. While all the pedagogical work occurs in schools, only
the district headquarters can lead the effort to translate state standards
and tests so that students are taught the right content in an effective
sequence, complete with software and print materials that support the
academic goals. Only the district can maintain a comprehensive student database that collects classroom, school, district, and state data.
And only the district can conduct comparative analyses of schools and
classrooms to identify problems and pose the appropriate questions for
investigation and hypothesis. The district must employ supervisors who
recognize good teaching and can offer advice and hands-on assistance
to all teachers on how to improve classroom practices. Such profes-

sionals are in short supply; districts cannot wait on universities to stock the pipeline, but rather should identify or recruit proven talent aggressively. Otherwise, teachers are left to do what they do now, confirming Einstein's warning.

5. The educational chain of command has become corrupted by over-regulation, litigation, paperwork, and wheel-spinning.

Call it politics or call it culture, but recognize that the primary motivation of educational policymakers and bureaucrats is not to support teachers so that they can practice more effective pedagogy. Rather, their goals appear to be to satisfy a thirst for simplistic "solutions"; to explain away and excuse the lack of sustained improvements in student achievement; to reduce work to manageable and routine chunks, however unrelated to improved instruction they may be; and to protect the status quo. Paperwork, not a reflective professional culture, is the currency of exchange.

Pursuing pedagogical remedies through litigation can be particularly damaging, because the purported solution is mandated with the force of law. In various legal cases addressing educational challenges, judges have determined that the evidence presented permits them to determine how to close the intractable achievement gap, how to educate disabled students with multiple problems, what minimum size classrooms should be, and whether native-language instruction will or will not facilitate English-language acquisition. While litigation can help resolve issues of equity, it is precisely the wrong way to improve classroom practices.

Years of broken promises to change outcomes for kids validate this harsh conclusion. For poor, minority students the gap does not close, the educational payoffs are not made, their futures are not improved. The pattern of failure is so complete that addressing it is more than a bureaucratic or political issue—it is a moral obligation.

6. Educators have tried to universalize instruction and avoided sound pedagogy.

Vendors—whether they are professors, consultants, software producers, or textbook manufacturers—profit by doing the same thing over and over, even if it is unrelated to the needs of their customers. Professors dust off their notes from last year; consultants offer the same solutions to very diverse clients with very different problems; and software producers and textbook manufacturers reduce content to the lowest common denominator between Texas and California, their two largest markets. Such market forces serve as powerful drivers of our educational system, but they rarely serve the best interests of our students.

Many local educators assume that their instructional duties are defined by whatever reading series or math textbooks are adopted at the district level. Even after decades of evidence that textbooks are not an adequate base for educating American students to international standards or closing the achievement gap, their use remains close to universal.

If education funding is generous, as it is in New Jersey, superintendents who do not actually know how to improve instruction instead hide behind the purchase of new, "scientifically-based" learning programs, software, textbooks, supplemental services, and after-school packages. Principals and teachers can be overwhelmed by the introduction of unconnected and incoherent "innovations" far beyond their capacity to master and to implement in a short time.

7. Educational reformers have failed to recognize that those who need to change what they do must be involved in the process.

Reformers analyze, debate, confer, reanalyze, draft, write, and confer again. Those whose work is to be "reformed" are left out. Frequently, reformers mold their analyses of problems to fit their predetermined, sometimes ideologically driven, solutions. Pedagogy is almost always ignored. Instructional problems require the voluntary and engaged participation of teachers, principals, and supervisors. Relationships in public education are hierarchal: federal, state, local board, superintendent, principal, teacher, parent, student. They are not collegial or professional. The system relies on mandates, judicial rulings, compliance monitoring, regulations, statutes, and policy directives to set priorities, which are almost always irrelevant to what works in classrooms. Moreover, those who set the rules usually have little or no credibility as successful practitioners.

Change in classroom practice cannot be mandated from above, if it is to be effective. There must be agreement up and down the ranks about the character and magnitude of the problems to be addressed. This in itself calls for a level of professional candor that is not common among educators. There must be participation by teachers and administrators in determining what approaches hold the most promise for solving problems. And everyone should agree on the interim goals to be met, the evidence to be collected to see what is working, and the adjustments to be tried when something does not work.

In fact, this is a short description of what happens in poor districts whose students are closing the achievement gap.

What Works

Real pedagogy is what works. Education is a profession only when it is practiced like a profession. Otherwise, it is a trade. Doctors, dentists, accountants, and lawyers are paid to judge individual facts and circumstances against a body of accepted principles, laws, and/or research-proven practices and techniques. When educating children is reduced to scripted drills or the mechanical implementation of models, it ceases to be a profession. Restoring the basic professional principles of education leads to greatly improved results—at least, that is the lesson taught by New Jersey's experience since 2002.

Policy does matter. Policy should be clear and concrete. It should make plain and prioritize its objectives so that those who are to carry out the policy know that some mandated activities are more important than other mandated activities. If improved pedagogy is the goal, policy must support the conditions that will produce better teaching and learning.

The lesson learned in New Jersey is that, if educational policy is to close the achievement gap, it must focus on what works in the classroom. Specifically:

♦   Academic achievement trumps other important objectives.

♦   A clear set of ambitious academic goals must be set forth by grade level and content area. This responsibility belongs first to the state, then to the district.

♦   Within the broad area of academic achievement, priority must go to teaching primary grade students to read and write English well. This should be established with a sense of urgency, given that schools have only a few years to make certain that children can read by age nine.

◆ The district must keep track of the progress that each student is making in meeting academic goals. The primary way to determine such progress is regular, interim, district-designed assessments of essential academic standards, every eight weeks or so. District personnel must then help translate the results of these assessments into short-term instructional objectives for each student and teacher.

◆ When a student falls behind, there must be a system for rescuing him or her, which includes spending whatever additional time is required to bring that student up to par. The expense for such attention must take precedence over other spending demands.

◆ Teachers must be treated as front-line professionals who, of course, need continuous support in their efforts to improve their students' academic results. Any teacher in the first year on the job is an obvious candidate for particularly intensive attention.

◆ The process and set of practices must never end. Effective instruction involves constant adjustment, checks on how the adjusted instruction is working, and then (usually) readjustments.

◆ As students become literate in language and mathematics, the next step is to make school an engaging, fascinating experience. That means using diverse instructional materials that cut across content areas, and projects that showcase the wonder of learning.

◆ This is pretty simple stuff to describe, but very difficult to bring to life in thousands of classrooms. It is what happens in the nation's most successful city school district, Union City, as well as in other urban districts in New Jersey. It's called education.

New Jersey's Encouraging Story

Those who preach that American education should be "reformed" by way of a "systemic" reworking, and nothing less will do, are to be commended for not giving up. Usually, and unhappily for poor children in most districts, they provide answers to the wrong questions and ignore the implications of their "reforms" for students and teachers. Their efforts reward conference sites, publishers, consultants, academics, and foundation officials, but not the intended beneficiaries.

The New Jersey story told here concludes with optimism. Policy and practice can come together to focus relentless attention on the classroom and what happens there. We know by now that students rarely cooperate with the predictions of model-builders, and that teachers are exposed to a steady stream of unrealistic panacea and unhelpful oversight. However, if the management of school districts with concentrations of poor children will concentrate on addressing the pedagogical puzzles their students present, then impressive results are possible.

The most important lesson from New Jersey is that the restoration of pedagogy as the primary activity of schools, and the return of respect for the professionalism of those who oversee and teach in those schools, are the essential ingredients. The work to be done has been simply described above. One is hard-pressed to identify work that is more difficult.

11

Epilogue

Two important events that affect the *Abbott* effort to jump-start early literacy have occurred since the author departed the New Jersey Department of Education (NJDOE) in April 2007. First, the department was reorganized to better serve poor students not residing in Abbott districts. The consolidated functions of the Division of Abbott Implementation were distributed to other divisions: a new Division of Early Childhood Education; the division responsible for academic programs, standards, and testing; the division responsible for student services such as Title I and special education; and the finance division, for reviewing Abbott district budgets. After sixteen months or so, the effect of the new organization has been to greatly reduce the focus on early literacy.

Second, a new school aid formula was enacted that effectively eliminates the distinction between Abbott districts and other districts. Under the new strategy, the amount of state funding in current Abbott districts would be determined by the same formula applied to other districts: a base amount for "adequate" educational services, to which are added funds for every student who is classified as special education, as an English-language learner, or as eligible for free or reduced-price lunch. In a few Abbott districts, the formula produces significant funding increases; in most, it will require that local property taxes support more of the school budget, current expenditures be reduced, or a combination of the two. Parents of students not eligible for free or reduced-price lunches in Abbott districts would have to pay an income-based fee for preschool.

On November 18, 2008, the New Jersey Supreme Court decided that the Corzine administration had not demonstrated that its new formula would provide "a constitutionally adequate education" to Abbott district students. Not only did the court reject the administration's request to be relieved of the Abbott funding criteria, it awarded Abbott districts the opportunity to request additional funding beyond the formula. The case was remanded to a superior court judge for accelerated hearing and decision. The burden of proof is placed squarely on the Corzine administration.

One effect of the new formula is to greatly increase the number of school districts that must provide Abbott-quality preschool programs. The universe of such districts has risen from thirty-one to one hundred nine, and the universe of eligible three- and four year-old children has gone from 55,000 to approximately 85,000. The 2008–09 school year is designated a planning year for districts to identify their eligible students, determine if the district will provide some or all of the preschool classes, and to work with NJDOE on learning about preschool curricula and quality.

One of the least disputable lessons from the Abbott Division's focus on early literacy is that most school districts must be given intensive, continuous, tailored assistance by NJDOE if high-quality and efficient preschool is to be provided. Despite the enormous expansion in potential "customers" for such services, the Division of Early Childhood Education received no increase in staff. One must be pessimistic that the potential impact of expanded preschool will be realized with such a "penny wise, pound foolish" approach.

NOTES

CHAPTER 1

1. Massachusetts's fourth graders tested on NAEP broke down as 75 percent white, 8 percent black, 10 percent Latino, and 26 percent eligible for free or reduced price lunch; New Jersey's were 59 percent white, 15 percent black, 18 percent Latino, and 27 percent eligible for free or reduced price lunch. See Jihyun Lee, Wendy S. Grigg, and Patricia L. Donahue, *The Nation's Report Card: Reading 2007* (Washington, D.C.: National Center for Education Statistics, 2007), Table 7.

2. Ibid., Figure 10, p. 16; Table 7, p. 18; and Table A-9, p. 54.

3. This story ignores the "other gap," the one between American students and their peers in Singapore, Japan, Finland, Belgium, and other economically competitive nations.

4. Ibid., Table A-9, p. 54.

5. Ibid., Table A-16, p. 62.

CHAPTER 2

1. Jennifer N. Hochschild and Nathan Scovronick, *The American Dream and the Public Schools* (Oxford: Oxford University Press, 2003), p. 80.

2. Gary Orfield and Chungmei Lee, "Historic Reversals, Accelerating Resegration, and the Need for New Integration Strategies," Report to the Civil Rights Project, UCLA, August 2007, p. 20.

3. Betty Hart and Todd R. Risley, "The Early Catastrophe: The 30 Million Word Gap by Age 3," *American Educator,* Spring 2003.

4. Betty Hart and Todd R. Risley, *Meaningful Differences in the Everyday Experience of Young American Children* (Baltimore, Md.: Paul H. Brookes Publishing, 1995), pp. 198–99.

5. Steve Barnett, Julie Tarr, and Ellen Frede, "Early Childhood Needs in Low Income Communities," Center for Early Education Research, Rutgers University, New Brunswick, N.J., May 1999.

6. Jihyun Lee, Wendy S. Grigg, and Patricia L. Donahue, *The Nation's Report Card: Reading 2007* (Washington, D.C.: National Center for Education Statistics, 2007).

7. Orfield and Lee, "Historic Reversals, Accelerating Resegration, and the Need for New Integration Strategies," p. 11.

8. There is a second achievement gap—between the academic performance of U.S. students on international tests in science and mathematics and students from Asia and Europe, rivals for jobs and economic growth—that is not addressed directly.

9. Marianne Perie, Rebecca Moran, Anthony D. Lutkus, and William Tirre, "NAEP 2004 Trends in Academic Progress: Three Decades of Student Performance in Reading and Mathematics," National Center for Education Statistics, July 2005, pp. 33–35. Between 1971 and 1988, black thirteen- and seventeen-year-old students closed the gap in reading by about half, only to see it widen in subsequent years; black nine-year-olds have reduced the gap by about 40 percent over thirty-three years, but hardly at all since 1988. Nine-year-old Hispanic students scored slightly higher than their black peers, but thirteen- and seventeen-year-olds show very slight progress at closing the gap with white students, and it has grown wider since 1988.

10. Jihyun Lee, Wendy S. Grigg, and Gloria S. Dion, *The Nation's Report Card: Mathematics 2007* (Washington, D.C.: National Center for Education Statistics, 2007), pp. 8, 24.

11. Seymour B. Sarason, *The Predictable Failure of Educational Reform: Can We Change Course before It's Too Late?* (San Francisco: Jossey-Bass, 1990), p. 38.

12. James E. Coleman, *Equality of Educational Opportunity* (Washington, D.C.: Department of Health, Education, and Welfare, 1966).

13. See Ellen R. Delisio, "Department of Defense Schools: Their Secret Weapons for Success," *Education World,* May 30, 2007.

14. Ibid., p. 18.

15. Lee et al., *The Nation's Report Card*, Table A-9, p. 54.

16. What is most New Jersey–centric is that the state's supreme court decided the policies on both district funding and on giving three- and four-year-olds the opportunity for a high-quality preschool program, issues that may take longer and be resolved less tidily via the legislative process.

CHAPTER 3

1. "Price of everything . . ." borrowed from Oscar Wilde's Lord Henry in *The Picture of Dorian Gray*.

2. Commission on No Child Left Behind, "Beyond NCLB: Fulfilling the Promise to Our Nation's Children," The Aspen Institute, Washington, D.C., 2007, p. 118.

3. Gail L. Sunderman and Gary Orfield, "Domesticating a Revolution: No Child Left Behind Reforms and State Administrative Response," *Harvard Educational Review* 76, no. 4 (Winter 2006).

4. Jihyun Lee, Wendy S. Grigg, and Patricia L. Donahue, *The Nation's Report Card: Reading 2007* (Washington, D.C.: National Center for Education Statistics, 2007), pp. 11, 29.

5. U.S. Department of Commerce, Bureau of the Census, "Hispanic Population of the United States: 2004," Table 1.2.

6. See Douglas S. Massey, "When Less Is More: Border Enforcement and Undocumented Migration," Testimony to the Subcommittee on Immigration, Citizenship, Refugees, Border Security and International Law, Committee on the Judiciary, U.S. House of Representatives, April 20, 2007.

7. It is possible that some recently enacted statutes that reorganize large city districts may provide those districts with greater operational latitude than is seen in most state board of education regulations. The New York state law that placed the New York City schools under the mayor, for example, appears to permit fairly swift changes in school governance, while retaining any conditions of collectively bargained labor contracts.

CHAPTER 4

1. See Goodwin Liu, "How the Federal Government Makes Rich States Richer," p. 4, and Ross Wiener and Eli Pristoop, "How States Shortchange the Districts that Need the Most Help," p. 7, in "Funding Gaps 2006," The Education Trust, December 20, 2006.

2. The original Abbott districts were selected by an appendix to *Abbott II* (1990) that listed municipalities eligible for an urban aid program in 1977. They are: Asbury Park, Bridgeton, Burlington City, Camden, East Orange, Elizabeth, Garfield, Gloucester City, Harrison, Hoboken, Irvington, Jersey City, Keansburg, Long Branch, Millville, Neptune Township (since 1996), New Brunswick, Newark, Orange, Passaic, Paterson, Pemberton Township, Perth

Amboy, Phillipsburg, Plainfield (since 1996), Pleasantville, Salem City (since 2003), Trenton, Union City, Vineland, and West New York.

3. In *Abbott X* (2003), the court accepted a mediated agreement with the plaintiffs that shifted most of the *Abbott V* remedies from mandates to addressing "demonstrated need and effectiveness."

4. For a very readable and clear report on the evolution of the *Abbott* litigation, see Deborah Yaffe, *Other People's Children: The Battle for Justice and Equality in New Jersey's Schools* (New Brunswick, N.J.: Rutgers University Press, 2007).

5. Author's calculations using the state aid summaries and enrollment reports of the New Jersey Department of Education, available on its Web site, www.state.nj.us/education/data/.

6. "Summary of Vital Statistics," *Comparative Spending Guide 2007,* New Jersey Department of Education, March 2007, pp. 3-4, available online at http://www.state.nj.us/education/guide/2007/abbott.pdf.

7. Ben Dalton, Jennifer Sable, and Lee Hoffman, *Characteristics of the 100 Largest Public Elementary and Secondary School Districts in the United States: 2003–04* (Washington, D.C.: U.S. Department of Education, September 2006), pp. A-30–33.

Chapter 5

1. The author was, from 1998 to 2001, the president of Citizens for Better Schools, a nonprofit advocacy organization, and participated with the Education Law Center in the effort to change *Abbott*'s focus to closing the achievement gap and to improving the quality of preschool education.

2. The tenor and content of guidance, regulations, and presentations can be seen on the Web site of the NJDOE, specifically the archives of the Abbott district information, available online at http://www.nj.gov/education/abbotts/archives/. "Simplifying and Focusing: Abbott Work in 2005–06" is a useful example.

3. Jun Choi, a graduate of MIT and Columbia University, was recruited to organize the database (called NJ SMART) and to survey extant NJDOE data and collections. Even though the specifications for NJ SMART were drafted rather quickly, bureaucratic, political, and financial obstacles delayed its implementation. The first, small-scale data collections for NJ SMART took place in the 2007–08 school year. Choi left NJDOE to run for mayor

in Edison, a race he won at the age of thirty-four in the state's fifth-largest municipality.

4. In my previous position, I commissioned detailed statistical studies of the 2000 fourth grade literacy test results, which showed that virtually all Union City schools were at the eighty-fifth percentile or higher, as were half those in West New York.

5. Smaller, more affluent *Abbott* districts Garfield and Pemberton did slightly better than Perth Amboy, as did New Brunswick, which was smaller but just as poor.

6. In the official enrollment data collected by the NJDOE for the 2006–07 school year, 88.9 percent of all students were free-lunch eligible in Union City. The next highest Abbott district was Passaic, at 76.7 percent, followed by Asbury Park at 74.5 percent.

7. The use of fourth grade test results may be confusing, given the emphasis on third grade as a critical threshold for reading at grade level. Simply put, the third grade state test was not introduced until 2004, so the fourth grade results beginning in 1999 were the only data available.

8. Happily, the Union City leadership has built on the strong foundation that Carrigg helped build—its students continue to perform at high levels.

CHAPTER 6

1. See W. Steven Barnett, Jason T. Hustedt, Laura E. Hawkinson, and Kenneth B. Robin, *The State of Preschool 2006: State Preschool Yearbook* (New Brunswick, N.J.: National Institute for Early Education Research, 2006), p. 12.

2. See W. Steven Barnett, "Long-term Effects on Cognitive Development and School Success," in *Early Care and Education for Children in Poverty*, W. S. Barnett and S. S. Boocock, eds. (Albany, N.Y.: SUNY Press, 1998), pp. 11–44.

3. Barnett et al., *The State of Preschool*, pp. 102–06.

4. Interview with Ellen Frede, March 14, 2008.

5. Thelma Harms, Richard M. Clifford, and Debby Cryer, *Early Childhood Environment Rating Scale, Revised Edition* (New York: Teachers College Press, 1998).

6. W. Steven Barnett, Julie E. Tarr, Cindy Esposito Lamy, and Ellen C. Frede, "Fragile Lives, Shattered Dreams: A Report on Implementation of Preschool in New Jersey's *Abbott* Districts," Center for Early Education Research, New Brunswick, N.J., 2001, pp. 9–10.

7. For an accessible summary, see Barbara T. Bowman, M. Suzanne Donovan, and M. Susan Burns, eds., *Eager to Learn: Educating Our Preschoolers* (Washington, D.C.: National Research Council, 2001), Chapters 2–4.

8. Although not formally adopted by the NJBOE until 2004, these standards were used for planning professional development beginning in 2002. New Jersey Department of Education, *Preschool Teaching and Learning Expectations: Standards of Quality,* July 2004, available online at http://liberty.state.nj.us/education/ece/code/expectations/expectations.htm.

9. Ellen Frede, "Assessment in a Continuous Improvement Cycle: New Jersey's Abbott Preschool Program," Paper submitted to National Early Childhood Accountability Task Force, September 2005, pp. 5–9.

10. Ibid., pp. 9–11.

11. Ellen Frede, Kwanghee Jung, W. Steven Barnett, Cynthia Esposito Lamy, and Alexandra Figueras, "The Abbott Preschool Program Longitudinal Effects Study (APPLES)," Early Learning Improvement Consortium and New Jersey Department of Education, June 2007; enrollment data is on p. 5, teacher data on p. 10.

12. Ibid., pp.5–6

13 Ibid., p. 11.

14. Ibid, pp. 18–20.

15. Ibid., pp. 23–35.

16. Correspondence from Frank DeRiso, Union City Public Schools, September 14, 2007.

17. "Early childhood education" usually covers children from birth, or at least age three, through third grade; "preschool" is obviously covered within early childhood.

18. Maria Newman, "New Jersey to Provide Full-day Preschool in Its 28 Poorest Districts," *New York Times,* January 7, 1999.

19. Even though detailed and documented audits of probable criminal activity for five or six providers were shared with the attorney general, no indictments were brought until the Corzine administration in 2006.

20. NJAC 6A:26-3.11.

21. When Governor Whitman resigned to join the Bush administration as administrator for the Environmental Protection Agency in January 2001, Senate President Donald DiFrancesco became acting governor under the succession provisions of the state constitution. He concurrently remained Senate president.

22. The truce, which included the Education Law Center supporting the administration's request for a budgetary "timeout" in 2002, was solid on preschool issues for at least five years. On budget and K–12 mandates, the truce lasted about ten months.

23. Ellen Frede resigned in August 2006 to return to her faculty position at The College of New Jersey.

24. Gene I. Maeroff makes a convincing case that P–3 schools should replace conventional K–6 or K–8 elementary schools in *Building Blocks: Making Children Successful in the Early Years of School* (New York: Palgrave, 2006).

CHAPTER 7

1. *Abbott v. Burke,* 153 NJ 480(1998) at 19.

2. Ibid., at 21, 17.

3. Ibid., at 41 (emphasis added).

4. The NAS Request for Proposals is quoted in Henry F. Olds and Robert Pearlman, "Designing a New American School," *Phi Delta Kappan* 74, no. 4 (December 1992): 1–2 (emphasis added).

5. See Jeffrey Mirel, "The Evolution of the New American Schools: From Revolution to Mainstream," Thomas Fordham Foundation, Washington, D.C., October 2001, see discussion pp. 22–28.

6. *Abbott V, op.cit.* at 41.

7. Bari Anhalt Erlichson, "Comprehensive School Reform in New Jersey: Waxing and Waning Support for Model Implementation," *Journal of Education for Students Placed At Risk* 10, no. 1 (2004): 19.

8. Ibid., p. 21.

9. Despite assertions to the contrary, SFA was not well aligned with New Jersey's curriculum standards, or its tests, which gave 50 percent credit to writing on its language arts tests. SFA did not teach writing for the first six years or so. It was added to the ninety minutes prescribed for reading.

10. Bari Anhalt Erlichson and Margaret Goertz, "Implementing Whole School Reform in New Jersey: Year Two," Rutgers University, 2001, p. 63.

11. Author calculations from annual NJDOE reports for staffing and enrollment.

Chapter 8

1. According to the NJDOE, then, the skill for a fourth grader to "listen actively for a variety of purposes such as enjoyment." is to be taken just as seriously as the writing skill to "engage the reader . . . with an interesting opening, logical sequence, and satisfying conclusion." New Jersey Department of Education, "Core Curriculum Content Standards," Language Arts Literacy (October 2004), Standards 3.4 and 3.2.

2. Only 29 percent of Abbott fourth graders were proficient or advanced proficient on the 1999 language arts test; 32 percent on fourth grade math. Fifty-two percent of Abbott eighth graders were proficient on language arts, but only 30 percent on math.

3. Author calculations from Office of Special Education Programs, New Jersey Department of Education, "2007 Classification Rates by District, Age 3–21 as of December 1, 2007."

4. The twelve districts are Asbury Park, Bridgeton, Camden, East Orange, Elizabeth, Irvington, Jersey City, Newark, Orange, Paterson, and Pleasantville.

5. For thirty years, research has documented high-performing schools serving concentrations of poor children in otherwise low-performing districts. Ron Edmonds specified the correlates of "effective schools." See Ronald R. Edmonds, "Effective Schools for the Urban Poor," *Educational Leadership* 37 (October 1979): 15–27. The Education Trust identifies such schools, as do occasional profiles in the *New York Times* and other publications. Almost always, the distinguishing variable is the stable presence of an unusually devoted, demanding, energetic principal.

6. Beyond persuasion, NJDOE had few levers available to encourage the adoption of improved pedagogy. Those available were blunt, provocative, and signaled a breakdown in partnership. For example, after Paterson agreed to use funds to purchase books for classroom libraries, it failed to do so; NJDOE threatened to withhold the release of funds for the purchase of classroom libraries.

7. Long Branch, which chose to retain its modified Success for All model, was the single exception. Its fourth graders' proficiency percentage improved from the low 60s to the low 70s in the 2003 to 2007 period.

8. The free lunch data are from the official enrollment reports filed with NJDOE for the 2006–07 school year.

9. Garfield, more a working-class suburb than a poor city, was the only Abbott district where more than 80 percent of fourth graders were proficient; Long Branch, at 70.3 percent, had the highest percentage of advanced proficient students (6.8 percent).

CHAPTER 9

1. In the three districts selected as exemplars of good literacy practice, the classification rates for their fourth graders in 2007 were 12.8 percent in Perth Amboy, 11.1 percent in Union City, and 14.8 percent in West New York. The average for other Abbott districts was 15.6 percent.

2. New Jersey Department of Education, Office of Special Education Programs, "Special Education Data," 2007, available online at http://www.state.nj.us/education/special/data/2007.htm.

3. Lorraine M. McDonnell, Margaret J. McLaughlin, and Patricia Morison, eds., *Educating One and All: Students with Disabilities and Standards-Based Reform* (Washington, D.C.: National Academy Press, 1997), p. 55.

4. Ironically, Union City was one of two districts rejecting the special education literacy program in its first year.

5. Compared to an average proficiency rate of 26 percent among Abbott special education students, Vineland improved to 51.5 percent, Perth Amboy to 41.5 percent, Orange to 43.5 percent, Union City to 57 percent, and Long Branch to 44 percent.

6. Jennifer Hochschild and Nathan Scovronick, *The American Dream and the Public Schools* (New York: Oxford University Press, 2003), p. 149.

7. Ibid., p. 149.

8. Ibid., p. 152.

CHAPTER 10

1. Seymour B. Sarason, *The Predictable Failure of Educational Reform: Can We Change Course before It's Too Late?* (San Francisco: Jossey-Bass, 1990), pp. 28–29.

2. For example, national board certification for exemplary teaching, increased content mastery before certification, increasing practice teaching, more literacy training for teachers at all levels, more math and science content v. "how-to teach" courses, requirements for higher GPA, greater reciprocity among states.

3. Strong American Schools Web site, available at http://www.edin08.com/AboutUs.aspx. Their commendable effort was unsuccessful in the end because of the financial meltdown and economic nosedive came to dominate voter attention after the party convention.

Index

Note: page numbers followed by *f* refer to figures; those followed by *n* refer to notes with note number.

ABOUT THE AUTHOR

Gordon MacInnes, a fellow at The Century Foundation and lecturer at Princeton University's Woodrow Wilson School, has devoted four decades to government service and leadership on issues related to education, poverty, and urban living. Prior to joining The Century Foundation, he served from 2002 to April 2007 as assistant commissioner for Abbott implementation for the New Jersey Department of Education, where he oversaw a division that was created to coordinate the implementation of *Abbott v. Burke,* the nation's most prescriptive and sweeping state supreme court ruling on school finance, and to improve academic achievement in the state's poorest cities. From 1998 to 2002, he served as president of Citizens for Better Schools, a New Jersey–based nonprofit organization. He was a member of the New Jersey State Senate from 1994 to 1998. Prior to that, he served in the New Jersey General Assembly and held positions that included chief executive of the New Jersey Network, director of the Fund for New Jersey, a special assistant to Governor Richard J. Hughes, special assistant to the New Jersey commissioner of education, deputy director of the White House Task Force on the Cities, and director of program development for United Progress, Inc., the anti-poverty agency for Trenton, New Jersey. He is the author of *Wrong for All the Right Reasons: How White Liberals Have Been Undone by Race* (A Twentieth Century Fund Book published by NYU Press, 1996) and "Kids Who Pick the Wrong Parents and Other Victims of Voucher Schemes" (a Twentieth Century Fund/Century Foundation white paper, 1999). He has a B.A. from Occidental College and an M.P.A. from The Woodrow Wilson School, Princeton University, where he also served as a visiting senior fellow from 1976 to 1978 and again from 1998 to 1999. He has had numerous opinion pieces published in the *Newark Star-Ledger,* the *Record* of Hackensack, the *Daily Record* of Morris County, and the New Jersey section of the *New York Times.*